SECRET
JACKSONVILLE

A Guide to the Weird, Wonderful, and Obscure

Bill Delaney

Reedy Press
PO Box 5131
St. Louis, MO 63139
www.reedypress.com

Library of Congress Control Number: 2021935124
ISBN: 9781681063348

Design by Jill Halpin

All images are courtesy of the author unless otherwise noted.

Printed in the United States of America
21 22 23 24 25   5 4 3 2 1

Mine Katie ysaysama, utiba alifota ninaquituluta iyenotima, chiqua inifinano, nanemi hubuasota, aboquasiro manda, caqi chara natacatosintala.

(Translated from Timucua: Honored Katie the beautiful, the great traveler who accompanies me wandering, my otter wife, eternally loving, desiring to honor, this writing I offer to her.)

CONTENTS

INTRODUCTION

One thing about secrets: they're usually not secrets to everybody. One person's arcane mystery or groundbreaking finding is often another person's common knowledge. This has been a familiar story in Jacksonville since the 16th century, when Europeans showed up claiming to have "discovered" an area that had already been populated for thousands of years.

I see Jacksonville as a city of secrets. It's full of incredible history, incomparable stories, and one-of-a-kind spaces, but often they're little known to big swaths of the populace. This is unfortunate in many ways, but it also means you don't have to go very far to find something truly special—you just have to dig a little deeper or step a little farther off the trail. As a writer and lifelong Jaxson, I've spent most of my career digging into Jacksonville's hidden stories and places, and I'm still finding things I never knew.

This book is my attempt to tell a few of the underrepresented and underknown stories of Jacksonville, St. Augustine, Fernandina Beach, and the broader First Coast region. I hope it'll help you get started on your own adventures. Here you'll find secrets such as these:

- Underknown historical sites, such as Fort Mose, the site of the first free Black town in the present-day United States
- Quirky or unusual places and items, such as "Sexy Rexy," the city's foremost orange concrete dinosaur
- Well-known places with some hidden feature or story, such as the Wells Fargo Center and the steam locomotive buried beneath it
- Everyday places to which folklore has become attached, such as the old elementary school known as the "Devil's School" or the witch Wiccademous's grave

Whether you're a visitor, newcomer, or longtime resident, I hope you'll enjoy reading *Secret Jacksonville* as much as I've enjoyed writing it. And if you find something cool, let me know at TheJaxsonMag.com.

THE GREAT FIRE OF 1901—JACKSONVILLE'S GREATEST TRAGEDY

How did a historic tragedy shape a city for decades to come?

On May 3, 1901, sparks from a chimney ignited a pile of Spanish moss drying at the Cleaveland Fibre Factory in LaVilla. The fire soon spread to nearby houses, and the fire department did little to save the predominantly Black neighborhood. However, when the wind shifted east, it blew the fire into Downtown Jacksonville. Over the next eight hours, the conflagration destroyed 146 city blocks and more than 2,000 buildings. It is known to have killed at least seven people, possibly more, and it displaced thousands. The Great Fire of 1901 remains the third-worst urban fire in American history, after the Great Chicago Fire and the one that followed the 1906 San Francisco earthquake.

The experience of the fire profoundly reshaped Jacksonville. First, Downtown Jacksonville had to be entirely rebuilt. The city's buildings were mostly built of wood before the fire, but their replacements used fire-resistant brick and steel. Architects, most notably Henry John Klutho, designed many of the buildings in the Prairie School style pioneered by Frank Lloyd Wright. As a result, Jacksonville still has the largest collection of Prairie School buildings outside the Midwest.

MEMORIAL TO THE GREAT FIRE OF 1901

WHAT: A public art sculpture memorializing the Great Fire of 1901

WHERE: On the Riverwalk at Market Street and Coastline Drive in Downtown Jacksonville

COST: Free

PRO TIP: There's also a historical marker at James Weldon Johnson Park with more information on the fire.

Memorial to the Great Fire of 1901

The fire also reshaped the wider city. Downtown had been a major residential center before the fire. Afterward, many who had lived there relocated to surrounding neighborhoods such as Springfield, Riverside, and Eastside, driving explosive growth in those areas. Downtown transitioned into a primarily business and retail district, which it remains today.

In 2002, Jacksonville memorialized the tragedy with a new public art installation. The Cultural Council of Greater Jacksonville commissioned sculptor Bruce White to create the piece, a spire 40 feet tall symbolizing the city's rise from the ashes. It stands on the Northbank Riverwalk at the end of Market Street.

The monument stands at the site of the "Market Street Horror," where the fire trapped people on a dock, resulting in at least two deaths and possibly many more.

DUUUVAL!

How did a county's name become a battle cry?

Go to enough events, parties, or football games in Jacksonville, and you'll hear someone, somewhere shout "DUUUVAL!" Generally, this will be followed by other people returning the cry, sometimes repeatedly. The refrain has become part of the local culture, an auditory way of showing civic pride or support for the Jacksonville Jaguars. But, why?

By the 1980s, if not earlier, "Duval" emerged in local African American speech as a substitute for Jacksonville, similar to terms like "Jax," "The 904," or the sadly less-common "Da Bangem." Duval County, named for Florida Territory's first civilian governor William Pope Duval, consolidated with the City of Jacksonville to form one government in 1968, bringing all unincorporated land into the city limits and making Jacksonville the biggest city in terms of land area in the lower 48 states. A natural substitute for the city name, "DUVAL" became a rallying cry.

In the early 1990s, DJ Easy E popularized the chant when he adopted it for his spots on former local hip-hop and R&B station 92.7 The Beat. Easy E drew out the syllables and added an echo effect and used it to close segments. Before long, the chant was everywhere. Jacksonville Jaguars fans brought it to the stadium, and Jaguars linebacker Mike Peterson introduced it to national audiences during a 2004 Monday Night Football game when he warned the Pittsburgh Steelers, "welcome to Duval—prepare to be hit!" The team embraced the chant and have included it in their marketing,

---

Changing Perspectives was created by artists Eric Moed, Caila Moed, and Samuel Maddox in collaboration with Main Made Studios.

Changing Perspectives, *the DUUUVAL bike rack*

standardizing the spelling with three U's and making it a popular social media hashtag.

In 2019, the city funded an art installation paying tribute to the battle cry. Called "Changing Perspectives," the piece is a bike rack that spells out "DUUUVAL" when looked at from the right angle. Each section features inscriptions about aspects of Jacksonville's Black history.

CHANGING PERSPECTIVES (THE "DUUUVAL" SCULPTURE)

WHAT: A functional art bike rack

WHERE: The corner of Ocean and Bay Streets in Downtown Jacksonville

COST: Free

PRO TIP: Caveat photographer: you've got to stand in the street to see "DUUUVAL" from the right angle.

ST. JOHN'S CATHEDRAL: STRANGE ROADS AND POLTERGEISTS

Why is the street grid so weird around the cathedral?

The seat of the Episcopal Church's Diocese of Florida, St. John's Cathedral has a history dating back to the formation of Jacksonville's first Episcopal parish in 1834. In 1842, the parish constructed its first church building atop Billy Goat Hill, then the city's highest point. The northern part of the property was the Old City Burying Grounds, Jacksonville's earliest known cemetery. Unbeknownst to those who traverse Downtown today, the cemetery still exists, hidden beneath the streets and buildings.

In 1852 the city established what's now known as Old City Cemetery (see page 32) on Union Street. In 1859, the cathedral closed the Billy Goat Hill burying grounds, and according to records the graves were relocated to the new cemetery as development cropped up around the cathedral. For 100 years, those records were

ST. JOHN'S CATHEDRAL

WHAT: Historic Episcopal Cathedral

WHERE: 256 E Church St.

COST: Free

PRO TIP: Check out the gargoyles all around the cathedral.

The current Gothic Revival-style cathedral opened in 1906, as the previous incarnation had been lost to the Great Fire of 1901 (see page 2).

St. John's Cathedral

believed to be truthful. Then in 1960, a city work crew digging up the street behind the cathedral stumbled upon three skeletons. Most assumed a few bodies had simply been missed, but in 2001, a JEA utility crew found five more skulls, indicating that many more bodies lie under the hill than anyone ever thought.

It appears that when the cemetery closed, many graves were simply left behind when the tombstones were removed. Observant readers will note this is exactly the premise of the movie Poltergeist. If that film is any indication, nearby developments like the Cathedral Townhomes are certainly infested with angry specters.

St. John's Cathedral has impacted the city's landscape in another subtle way. When it was established, the city's street grid didn't yet extend to Billy Goat Hill. When the city expanded the grid, it had to build streets around the church, resulting in a permanent quirk where the church sits in the middle of Market Street, with roads cutting around it.

CHAMBLIN'S, A BOOKLOVER'S LABYRINTH

Where can you peruse millions of used books?

Ron Chamblin's stores aren't so much a secret in themselves, but millions of secrets are contained within their maze-like walls. With 33,000 square feet of space and an estimated 3.5 million books between its locations, it's by far the biggest independent bookstore in Northeast Florida and among the biggest anywhere.

CHAMBLIN BOOKMINE AND CHAMBLIN'S UPTOWN

WHAT: The largest independent bookstore in Northeast Florida

WHERE: Chamblin Bookmine: 4551 Roosevelt Blvd.

Chamblin's Uptown: 215 N Laura St.

COST: Free

PRO TIP: It's easy to get lost in Chamblin Bookmine. Ask the front desk for a map.

Chamblin started out humbly in 1976 when he purchased the collection of Crawford's Bookmine. Cy Crawford had run his bookshop out of his Lakeshore home until a fire forced him to close. Chamblin paid $7,500 for 15 boxes of smoky books and the Bookmine name, and opened up his own used book shop on Herschel Street in the Fairfax neighborhood south of Avondale.

Chamblin Bookmine was a hit, and by 1987, the business had outgrown its location. Chamblin moved up the street in 1987 only to outgrow that space as well. In 1991, he purchased a much larger, 15,000-square-foot building off Roosevelt Boulevard. Within three years, this space was filled too, turning the interior into a vast literary labyrinth not unlike the library from *The Name of the Rose*. In 2004, Chamblin bought a nearby abandoned preschool building and connected it as an annex, adding another 8,000 square feet and all but ensuring that customers would get lost, generally happily, among the books.

Top: *Chamblin's Uptown on Laura Street.* Inset: *Inside Chamblin Bookmine on Herschel Street.*

In 2006, Chamblin expanded again, this time purchasing a second location. Chamblin's Uptown opened in a 12,000-square-foot building constructed in 1904 on Downtown's Laura Street. The Downtown store features a cafe and two stories of aisles and has become just as much of an institution as its predecessor.

Chamblin's Uptown is decorated with a distinctive fantasy mural by Jacksonville artist Shaun Thurston.

DUVAL BASS: THE MIAMI BASS SOUND IN JACKSONVILLE

Will you ride the train?

In the mid-1980s, a new sound emerged in South Florida's hip-hop scene. Immersed in the electro beats of early New York hip-hop and armed with Roland TR-808 drum machines, Miami DJs experimented with excessively low bass and raw, danceable rhythms. Rappers added vocal tracks, primarily about sex and partying, and Miami bass was born.

Popularized across South Florida by figures such as Uncle Luke and 2 Live Crew, by the late 1980s, Miami bass had blasted its way up I-95 to Central Florida, Jacksonville, and Georgia. In the early 1990s, Jacksonville produced a succession of successful Miami bass acts, all connected to the same production team: Jay Ski (Johnny McGowan) and C. C. Lemonhead (Nathaniel Orange). Known as Bass Mechanics and later as Quad City DJ's ("quad" was '90s Florida slang for bass), the duo realized they could take bass music to new heights of popularity if they toned down the vulgar lyrical content and turned up the production values.

In 1993, the duo formed the group 95 South, who released the Top-10 single "Whoot, There It Is," which predated a similarly named hit, Tag Team's "Whoomp

TRIBUTE TO JACKSONVILLE'S MIAMI BASS PIONEERS

WHAT: Part of an art installation by Karen Kurycki celebrating Jacksonville music

WHERE: Northwest corner of Bay and Liberty Streets in the Downtown Northbank

COST: Free

PRO TIP: Post a video at the installation with one of the groups' songs playing for instant Duval cred.

Public art celebrating Jacksonville's Miami bass acts

(There It Is)," by a month. When the group's vocalists departed, Jay Ski and Lemonhead formed a new outfit, 69 Boyz. In 1994 this group scored an even bigger hit, "Tootsee Roll." The following year, the DJ's produced the hit single "Freak Me Baby" for Dis-N-Dat, a sister duo from Atlanta. In 1996, the Quad City DJ's added vocalist JeLana LaFleur and found two more major hits under their own moniker, "C'mon N' Ride It (The Train)" and the theme song to the movie *Space Jam*.

Though their popularity waned after that, Jay Ski and Lemonhead left a mark on hip-hop as the biggest commercial success in the Miami bass scene. Today, an installation on Bay Street celebrates Jacksonville's contribution to the subgenre.

Karen Kurycki's installations commemorating local music are just a few of the public art pieces you can see Downtown. Check out visitjacksonville.com to take a self-guided tour.

THE TRAIN BURIED BENEATH A SKYSCRAPER

Is a locomotive sealed away beneath the Wells Fargo Center?

When it opened in 1974, the 37-floor Independent Life Building— now the Wells Fargo Center—immediately became one of Jacksonville's most recognizable structures. The tallest building in Florida until 1981 and the tallest in Jacksonville until 1990, it remains a dominant feature of the city's skyline. But even the most conspicuous landmarks have their secrets. In the Wells Fargo Center's case, there's a big one: a steam locomotive is buried beneath its foundation.

A longstanding rumor held that the building crew had found an old steam engine buried in the earth, but this was generally dismissed as an unproven urban legend. Then, in 2017, an eyewitness confirmed the story. In 1971, John C. Christian was a 17-year-old employee of Raymond International, the company contracted to build the skyscraper's foundation. The project required excavating 30 feet of earth to reach the bedrock below. Christian worked as a "gofer" for his uncle, the project supervisor, meaning he was often among the first to see what workers came across as they dug.

Fifteen feet down, the excavators hit a vein of black char: the residue of the Great Fire of 1901 (see page 2). Within that layer, the drills struck metal, revealing an incredible find: a locomotive. Given its place in the strata, Christian reckons it must have been a casualty

According to John Christian, the line of char they uncovered from the Great Fire of 1901 still smelled of fire when they uncovered it more than 70 years later.

The Wells Fargo Center

WELLS FARGO CENTER

WHAT: Jacksonville's second-tallest building

WHERE: 1 Independent Dr.

COST: Free

PRO TIP: Some downtown streets have traces of old railroad and streetcar tracks.

of the Great Fire. At that time, a rail line serving the city's many wharves ran along Bay Street, then at the river's edge. The engine may have been derailed by the fire and subsumed in mud and water.

Whatever the case, the crew recovered the engine's bell and other artifacts as they called in the bigwigs. Afraid that a media furor might delay the job, the bosses ordered the engine covered up, and construction continued around it. There it remains, sealed beneath one of Jacksonville's signature skyscrapers.

DOWNTOWN'S UNDERGROUND TUNNELS

Where can you go underground in Jacksonville?

A common myth holds that Jacksonville's terrain and high water table disallow basements. But not only do many Downtown buildings have basements, they were once connected by a lost web of subterranean tunnels. Unseen and unknown by most of the city, some of these tunnels can be found today.

In Downtown Jacksonville, the tunnels were built in the early 20th century to connect the banks headquartered there. They allowed money to be physically transferred to underground vaults or between buildings without risking robbery on the street. Seldom seen by the public, these passageways entered the realm of urban legend, especially when they became obsolete and were largely sealed off.

Some of the beautiful old vault doors still exist beneath the ground. One old tunnel remains in use today, running beneath Forsyth Street from the Atlantic National Bank Building to the BB&T Bank Building. Originally built for transferring cash, it was later adapted as a pedestrian walkway for employees when the Atlantic National Bank had offices in both buildings. The tunnel even had retail spaces, including a small restaurant that operated beneath the street from 1985 to 2015.

DOWNTOWN'S SECRET TUNNELS

WHAT: Subterranean passageways connecting Downtown buildings

WHERE: The only accessible tunnel runs beneath the Atlantic National Bank Building and the BB&T Bank Building.

COST: Free

PRO TIP: The tunnel can be found just to the left through the Atlantic National Bank Building's entrance.

Inside the tunnel beneath Forsyth Street

There are also tunnels under the Prime Osborn Convention Center, which was the Jacksonville Union Terminal station, one of the South's busiest train stations, from 1919 to 1974. Here the tunnels served to take passengers underneath the tracks from the main concourse to five outlying platforms. This design made all of the station's 26 tracks accessible from a single entrance without requiring passengers to cross the tracks. After the station closed, the tunnels were walled off and abandoned, and they are now flooded by water from nearby McCoys Creek. They remain a popular haunt of urban explorers.

Ad Lib Tours hosts walking tours that visit the tunnels. Book a reservation at adlibtours.com.

FORT CAROLINE ENGRAVINGS AT THE JACKSONVILLE MAIN LIBRARY

A series of 16th-century engravings are a window into Jacksonville's Native American past—or are they?

Jacksonville may be the only place in the continental US for which a substantial visual record exists from the mid-16th century. This record, such as it is, is attributed to Jacques le Moyne, the official painter for the French colony of Fort Caroline, founded in present-day Jacksonville in 1564.

Serving under commander René Goulaine de Laudonnière, Le Moyne's task was to create maps and images depicting the local Mocama Timucua society. In 1565, the Spanish sacked Fort Caroline and massacred the French. Le Moyne barely escaped with his life, and, with a small number of survivors, he managed to reach the ships and return to Europe. There's no indication any artworks made it out with him.

In 1591, Flemish engraver Theodor de Bry published Le Moyne's account of Fort Caroline, illustrated with 43 engravings he said were based on Le Moyne's paintings of the New World. De Bry stated that he purchased the manuscript and paintings from Le Moyne's widow after his death in 1588. Given the unlikelihood of original paintings surviving, any images Le Moyne made would have been later recreations. As many of the engravings depict the Mocama and other Timucua with whom the French interacted, they have

To learn more about the Mocama Timucua and the French settlement in Jacksonville, visit the Fort Caroline National Memorial.

FORT CAROLINE ENGRAVINGS AT THE JACKSONVILLE MAIN LIBRARY

WHAT: Series of 43 engravings by Theodor de Bry, claimed to be based on lost paintings by Jacques le Moyne

WHERE: The Jacksonville Public Library's Jordan and Shirley Ansbacher Gallery, 303 N Laura St.

COST: Free

PRO TIP: Also in the library is the Map Room, featuring dozens of maps of Florida from throughout history.

long been considered a valuable resource on the Timucua during this period.

In the 21st century, scholars have come to question de Bry's images. The images contain many errors: mountains in Florida, non-native shells, and weapons and clothing unlike any known in Florida. Some modern scholars believe de Bry embellished Le Moyne's work, while others doubt Le Moyne ever painted Florida at all.

But even as flawed sources, the engravings have value as an early and influential record of how Europeans envisioned Florida. The Jacksonville Public Library acquired copies of the engravings as part of the Ansbacher Map Collection. The images are on display in a dedicated hall in the special collections area.

OSSACHITE: A LOST TIMUCUA CITY?

Did a Timucua metropolis once stand at what's now Downtown Jacksonville?

T. Frederick Davis's 1925 book *The History of Jacksonville, Florida and Vicinity* mentions an evocative fact about Jacksonville's prehistory: old sources indicate that a Native American town stood at what's now Downtown. Davis further says that an old map (he doesn't say which) identifies a Timucua town called "Ossachite" at what could be modern Downtown.

Following Davis, many histories and guides to Jacksonville include Ossachite as the Timucua precursor to Jacksonville, often making far grander claims about it than Davis did. Today, sources allege that Ossachite was an important Timucua metropolis with thousands of residents. In 1931, a historical marker was placed at Ossachite's supposed location.

However, none of the many French or Spanish records for the area mention Ossachite, although they reference dozens of other towns. In the 16th century, the primary town of the Mocama Timucua was Saturiwa in Arlington, and later the mission settlement of San Juan del Puerto on Fort George Island (see page 84). Archaeologists have never found a substantial native settlement at Downtown Jacksonville.

So what was Ossachite? Timucua researcher Doug Henning and I have a theory: it likely comes from Frederick Davis's misreading of an

Explore authentic Timucua history at the Timucuan Preserve (page 152), or the Museum of Science and History. For other entertaining falsehoods, see the Fort Caroline engravings (page 16).

Top: *Plaque showing the location of the nonexistent Timucua city of Ossachite.* Bottom: *Pieter van der Aa's 1706 map showing Ossachile in an area that could appear to be Jacksonville.*

MARKER FOR THE SUPPOSED LOCATION OF OSSACHITE

WHAT: A 1931 historical marker of the (likely nonexistent) location of a Timucua city

WHERE: On the State Attorney's Office property at the northwest corner of Julia and Monroe Streets.

COST: Free

PRO TIP: Another out-of-date historical marker relevant to Native American history can be found at the northeast corner of Ocean and Monroe streets.

old map. A 1684 map of Florida by Jean B. L. Franquelin features the town of "Ossachile." Also known as Uzachile, in the 16th century this was the capital of a different Timucua people, the Yustaga, who lived in the Florida Panhandle. Franquelin's confused geography became even more confused in a later map based on it by Pieter van der Aa, which places Ossachile in an area that could indeed appear to be the location of Jacksonville. In our opinion, Davis simply misread Ossachile as Ossachite on van der Aa's map and inadvertently created a misunderstanding that survives a century later.

19

LaVilla, THE HARLEM OF THE SOUTH

How did LaVilla become an epicenter of African American life and culture?

Located immediately west of the Downtown Northbank, LaVilla emerged as Jacksonville's premier African American district after the Civil War. Initially an independent town, it was annexed by Jacksonville in 1887. Anchored by the Jacksonville Union Terminal, it became a hub of Black cultural life that's remembered fondly as the "Harlem of the South."

Among the notables who called LaVilla home were James Weldon Johnson and John Rosamond Johnson (see page 23) and Ma Rainey, the "mother of the blues." LaVilla was Florida's premier stop on the Chitlin Circuit, a series of African American performance venues throughout the country. LaVilla venues such as the Globe (now the Clara White Mission, see page 26), the Lenape, and the Ritz Theatre (see page 22) attracted talent such as Jelly Roll Morton, Billie Holiday, Duke Ellington, Ray Charles, and Louis Armstrong. Performers stayed in prestigious African American hotels, including the Richmond and the Wynn, located above the Lenape in what's now known as Genovar's Hall.

LaVilla's significance to music can't be overstated. The first recorded instance of blues singing in history occurred at LaVilla's Colored Airdome on Ashley Street in 1910. Oddly, the performer was a ventriloquist, John W. F. Woods, whose dummy Henry entertained

---

LaVilla residents such as the Johnson brothers and Ma Rainey contributed so much to the Harlem Renaissance that perhaps Harlem should be known as the LaVilla of the North.

Remains of Genovar's Hall in LaVilla

GENOVAR'S HALL

WHAT: Former jazz club and hotel

WHERE: 638 W Ashley St.

COST: Free

PRO TIP: Check out the Ritz Theatre and Museum for exhibits on LaVilla's golden age.

audiences by singing the blues. The Rabbit's Foot Company, the largest Black vaudeville troupe, was founded in LaVilla by Jacksonville native Pat Chapelle in 1900. Blind Blake, a blues and ragtime guitarist who lived in Jacksonville, recorded the song "Ashley Street Blues" about LaVilla's main strip in 1926.

LaVilla declined after the 1960s as many older residents left for new lives in the recently desegregated suburbs. Sadly, in the early 1990s, the city demolished most of the neighborhood in an ill-fated urban renewal plan. While the "Harlem of the South" is now barely recognizable, some historic structures stand today as reminders of its lost legacy.

RITZ THEATRE AND MUSEUM

Where can you learn the history of the "Harlem of the South"?

In the early 20th century, Jacksonville's LaVilla neighborhood (page 20) was known as the "Harlem of the South," a center of Black cultural life in the city. Home to leading lights such as brothers James Weldon Johnson and John Rosamond Johnson, the neighborhood contained a high concentration of theaters, music halls, and performance venues. Built in 1929, the Ritz Theatre was one of the city's finest movie houses for African Americans.

The Ritz building was designed in a unique combination of Egyptian revival, Mediterranean revival, and art deco styles by local architect Jefferson D. Powell. It was built by four local businessmen, including Joseph Hackel, who eventually became sole owner. It featured a one-screen theater with 970 seats and a highly decorated corner wall at Davis and State Streets with a large neon sign. In addition to showing movies, the theater hosted live performances and was the primary African American performance venue in LaVilla at the time. Like other theater buildings of the day, it also featured apartments and retail bays.

The Ritz Theatre served LaVilla through the 1960s, but its use declined along with the neighborhood around it. It eventually shut

---

RITZ THEATRE AND MUSEUM

WHAT: Performance venue and museum dedicated to Jacksonville's Black history

WHERE: 829 N Davis St.

COST: Standard admission is $9.70 for adults, and $6.65 for children, seniors, and military.

PRO TIP: The Ritz hosts regular performances. Check out its schedule for dates.

The Ritz Theatre and Museum

down and fell into disrepair. In the early 1990s, much of LaVilla was razed in an urban renewal plan, but the Ritz was bought by the City of Jacksonville. Most of the building was demolished and rebuilt, but the decorated corner wall was preserved. The new building serves as the Ritz Theatre and Museum. It features a 426-seat theater that hosts music, dance, and theater performances as well as a museum dedicated to the story of LaVilla and Jacksonville's Black history. One memorable exhibit features animatronic versions of James Weldon Johnson and John Rosamond Johnson, who discuss their lives and careers.

The Ritz Theatre's Johnson brothers exhibit was built by Sally Dark Rides, an animatronics company located just a few blocks away (see page 30).

LIFT EV'RY VOICE AND SING PARK: BIRTHPLACE OF AN ANTHEM

Where was the song known as the Black national anthem written?

This unassuming space in LaVilla is the birthplace of two of Jacksonville's most accomplished sons: James Weldon Johnson and J. Rosamond Johnson. Rosamond was a virtuoso pianist who toured widely. James was, among other things, principal of Stanton School, which he converted into Florida's first Black high school; a US consul; a Harlem Renaissance leader; the first Black head of the NAACP; and the celebrated author of works such as *The Autobiography of an Ex-Colored Man*.

In the house that once stood in this space in 1900, the brothers wrote one of their greatest works: the hymn "Lift Ev'ry Voice and Sing." For a celebration of Abraham Lincoln's birthday, the brothers composed the song for the children's choir. James wrote the lyrics in a poetic ecstasy, while Rosamond set them to music. The song, which invokes both the adversity African Americans had faced and their perseverance in striving for a better future, was an instant hit. The children who sang it taught it to others, and before long, it had spread across the country, becoming recognized as the "Black national anthem."

Among those inspired by the hymn was Green Cove Springs-born sculptor Augusta Savage. When the 1939 New York World's Fair

LIFT EV'RY VOICE AND SING PARK

WHAT: A park on the space where James Weldon Johnson and J. Rosamond Johnson were born

WHERE: 120 Lee St.

COST: Free

PRO TIP: Check out the Harp mural near James Weldon Johnson Park for a modern take on Augusta Savage's masterpiece.

Top: *Lift Ev'ry Voice and Sing Park in 2021, before development commenced.* Inset: *Tribute to Augusta Savage's "Lift Every Voice and Sing" in Downtown Jacksonville.*

commissioned her to sculpt a piece, she chose "Lift Ev'ry Voice and Sing" as inspiration. Her masterpiece, "The Harp," took the form of a huge instrument with choir singers as its strings. A plaster version debuted at the exhibition, but, unfortunately, money for a bronze version never materialized, and the original was demolished when the fair closed in 1940.

The Johnson homesite sat vacant for decades, but in 2015, it was dedicated as a city park, with plans to develop it into a proper tribute for the Johnson brothers. Fittingly, the plans, which were fully funded in 2021, include a bronze re-creation of Savage's lost masterpiece "The Harp."

The park's development is spearheaded by the Jessie Ball DuPont Fund, the City of Jacksonville, Durkeeville Historical Society, and donors. For updates on the progress, visit dupontfund.org/levs.

CLARA WHITE MISSION

How did a classic music hall become a sanctuary for the needy?

Providing meals, housing, and workforce training to the homeless and underserved across Jacksonville, the Clara White Mission has been a major humanitarian institution in Jacksonville for more than a century. Its building on Ashley Street in LaVilla, once the epicenter of African American culture in Northeast Florida (see page 20), has a storied history that predates the venerable mission.

The initial building dates to 1908, when the Bijou Theater opened as the first theater on Ashley Street. A three-story building with a movie theater and stage for vaudeville shows, it was renovated as the Globe Theater in 1910. The Globe was a major stop for touring performers, and its stock company was one of the largest African American troupes in the country. Among the Globe Stock Company's members was vocalist Gertrude "Ma" Rainey, who became known as the "Mother of the Blues." The Globe Theater closed in 1916, unable to compete with newer theaters.

CLARA WHITE MISSION

WHAT: Nonprofit headquarters

WHERE: 613 W Ashley St.

COST: Free (donations are welcome)

PRO TIP: Contact the mission to visit the Eartha M. M. White museum.

White Harvest Farms (page 54) is another initiative of the Clara White Mission. Eartha White earlier used the area as a swimming pool for African Americans.

The Clara White Mission

Meanwhile, philanthropist Eartha M. M. White formally organized the Clara White Mission to provide food for the needy in 1904. It was named for her mother Clara White, who had been feeding people from her Clay Street home since the 1880s. During the Great Depression in the 1930s, the need for the mission's services grew so much that White had to find a new location. In 1934, she purchased the old Globe Theater. In addition to the original hunger relief program, the new Clara White Mission headquarters included rooms, job training, clothing donations, and offices. In the 1930s, African Americans working for the Works Project Administration's Florida Writers Project were based in the mission; Zora Neale Hurston (see page 36) worked there in 1939.

Eartha White lived on the second floor of the building until her death in 1974. Her quarters are now a museum of her life and work, displaying the furniture and objets d'art she collected over her life.

THE WHETSTONIAN

What is Jacksonville's greatest work of outsider art?

Throughout his 81 years, Walter Whetstone collected unusual and unappreciated curios, artworks, and relics that others had discarded. From the 1990s until his death in 2018, he lovingly installed them in and around his LaVilla property, which he named the Whetstonian. "If Smithson can have his Smithsonian," he would tell visitors, "then Whetstone can have the Whetstonian."

The Whetstonian comprises a two-story commercial building built in 1927, a 1965 insurance office, and a lot connecting them. The 1927 building dates to LaVilla's heyday as the epicenter of African American cultural life in Jacksonville (see page 20). It was originally a mixed-use building with two apartments above commercial storefronts, which over the years hosted businesses that included a grocery store, an apothecary, a pool hall, and restaurants. Whetstone, an insurance agent by trade, purchased the buildings in the 1990s to spare them from being razed in an urban renewal project that flattened most of LaVilla.

THE WHETSTONIAN

WHAT: Home bedecked with discarded items

WHERE: 801 N Jefferson St.

COST: Free

PRO TIP: Make sure to circle the whole block to see everything the Whetstonian has to offer.

For a different view of LaVilla's long and storied past, check out the Ritz Theatre and Museum (see page 22).

The Whetstonian

Soon, the half-block complex was bedecked inside and out with Whetstone's collection, which included musical instruments, African statues, signs, old glass bottles, antique lamps, and mannequin pieces, among many other things. Whetstone found most of it in the city's African American neighborhoods, especially LaVilla. In bringing them all to the Whetstonian, Whetstone did something more than build an informal museum of the city's forgotten things. Many commenters have described the Whetstonian itself as outsider art, a work by someone not formally trained or part of the art world but still achieving its own significance.

Since Whetstone's death, his wife and family have maintained it, and there have been talks of landmarking the buildings. For now, Jacksonville's largest and greatest work of outsider art still stands proud, ready to share with passersby a million forgotten pieces of history.

SALLY DARK RIDES

Why is there a robotics factory in the middle of Downtown Jacksonville?

The unusual warehouse at 745 W. Forsyth St. is home to an even more unusual tenant: Sally Dark Rides, a manufacturer of animatronics (basically robotic puppets) and amusement park attractions. In business since 1977, Sally has evolved into the world's leading independent creator of dark rides, a type of indoor ride where vehicles carry guests through immersive scenes—think Disney's Pirates of the Caribbean.

SALLY DARK RIDES

WHAT: Amusement ride factory

WHERE: 745 W Forsyth St.

COST: Free

PRO TIP: Book a free tour at sallydarkrides.com.

Sally got its start in local dentist John Rob Holland's garage, where he and John Fox built custom animatronic figures, including "Sally," a character developed for dental presentations. In 1977, they brought in John Wood to turn their shop into a full-fledged business, and they began building mechanical mannequins for stores and displays.

Sally has flourished where competitors failed by continually improving its products and pivoting to meet current demands. When the novelty of animatronic store displays wore off, Sally moved on to musical shows for restaurants hoping to emulate Chuck E. Cheese. When singing animals became passe, they

For more than 40 years, Sally Dark Rides tours have been a unique experience for visitors, school groups, and company retreats.

Left: *Inside Sally's animatronics factory.*
Inset: *Sally Dark Rides.*

shifted fully to dark rides and pioneered the use of interactive "shooting gallery" elements where guests can aim for targets and rack up points as they ride.

Sally Dark Rides' clients include major theme parks such as Six Flags and Legoland, but the company also serves smaller parks and attractions across the world. They rose above the competition by offering a "turnkey" product where they design, build, and install the entire ride, allowing smaller companies without the design resources of major parks to purchase high-quality rides. Locally, Sally Dark Rides built the robotic James Weldon Johnson featured at the Ritz Theatre Museum (see page 22). For those who want a behind-the-veil look at how dark rides make their magic or just want to see something they won't find anywhere else, Sally offers tours of its warehouse.

LAURA ADORKOR KOFI MAUSOLEUM

Why is a Ghanaian saint buried in Jacksonville's Old City Cemetery?

Founded in 1852 as Jacksonville's first public burial ground, Old City Cemetery contains thousands of graves of early citizens, from mayors to soldiers to plain folks. Perhaps the cemetery's most striking feature is the white mausoleum by the back gate, where a saint lies interred.

Born the daughter of a king in Ghana in 1893, Laura Adorkor Kofi was, according to her followers, a prophet, social reformer, and "Warrior Mother of Africa's Warriors of the Most High God." She came to North America around 1918 and joined the United Negro Improvement Association (UNIA), a major Black nationalist organization founded by Marcus Garvey.

Kofi's charismatic orations soon attracted a dedicated following, and, in 1927, she relocated to Jacksonville to continue her work. Traveling across Florida, she drew thousands to her speeches. Her popularity earned her enemies within UNIA, and Garvey himself denounced her as a fraud in February 1928.

Kofi founded her own organization, the African Universal Church, headquartered in Jacksonville. The church attracted 25,000 active members, and Kofi's influence in Florida soon rivaled that of UNIA. On March 8, 1928, while Kofi preached to a packed Miami hall, an assassin's bullet struck and killed her. The crowd caught a Garvey follower and promptly beat him to death; police arrested his two associates, though neither were convicted.

The land that was once Adorkaville, named for Laura Adorkar Kofi, lies off Dabula Drive in Northwest Jacksonville.

Mausoleum of Laura Adorkor Kofi

LAURA ADORKOR KOFI MAUSOLEUM

WHAT: Tomb of the founder of the African Universal Church

WHERE: Off East Union Street near Washington Street

COST: Free

PRO TIP: Also buried in Old City Cemetery are Clara and Eartha White, founders of the Clara White Mission (see page 26).

Followers brought Kofi's body back to Jacksonville, stopping for funeral ceremonies that drew thousands in cities along the way. Final rites were held August 17 at Old City Cemetery, where 10,000 mourners gathered to see her laid to rest. The African Universal Church she founded regards her as a saint and considers the anniversary of her death a sacred day. The church spread outside of Florida and it founded a commune named Adorkaville off Old Kings Road in 1944. The community is gone now, and the congregations have declined, but "Mother Kofi's" memory still endures.

CAT HOUSE:
THE JAGUAR MURAL

What became of the iconic mural that once prowled Bay Street?

For 20 years, an abandoned Downtown building was home to one of Jacksonville's best-known pieces of site-specific art: a mural of a jaguar staring down passersby from the windows. Displaced by a long-awaited renovation, *Cat House* has found another home off the beaten path.

The Downtown Enhancement Committee commissioned the mural in 1995 to celebrate the inaugural season of the Jacksonville Jaguars. The Jags' arrival was a huge morale boost for a city that too often devalued and disparaged itself. Tapping an upswing of civic pride, the committee hoped to turn a vacant eyesore into an artistic canvas.

The Bostwick Building stands at a prominent location at the corner of Ocean and Bay Streets. Built the year after the Great Fire of 1901 (see page 2), the former bank building had been vacant since the early 1980s and allowed to deteriorate. For the mural, the committee engaged two local artists, Jim Draper and Anne Banas. They painted 23 plywood panels covering the windows, creating the image of an immense jaguar looking out. *Cat House* was an immediate hit with fans and soon became one of the most popular works of art in the city.

CAT HOUSE MURAL

WHAT: A mural of an enormous jaguar, created to fit the windows of the formerly abandoned Bostwick Building

WHERE: The J. Wayne and Delores Barr Weaver Center for Community Outreach, 616 A Philip Randolph Blvd.

COST: Free

PRO TIP: Mornings and late afternoons generally have the best lighting for pictures.

Jim Draper and Anne Banas's Cat House

The mural remained in place for the next 20 years as the Bostwick building continued to languish. In 2014, the city took possession of the building for back taxes and sold it to local businessman Jacques Klempf. Klempf put millions of dollars into the building, transforming it into the upscale Cowford Chophouse. However, the renovation displaced *Cat House*.

Fortunately, being painted on window coverings, the mural didn't have to be destroyed. Draper removed the panels and found a new, especially fitting place for them on the Eastside: FreshMinistries' Weaver Center for Community Outreach, named after its patrons, original Jaguars owner Wayne Weaver and his wife Delores.

There are two Jaguars looking out, as they were painted on both the Bay Street and Ocean Street sides of the Bostwick Building.

ZORA NEALE HURSTON IN THE FIRST COAST

What impact did Zora Neale Hurston have on Jacksonville—and vice versa?

Though she's primarily associated with her childhood home of Eatonville, famed author Zora Neale Hurston made the First Coast her home at various times throughout her life. Her first stint in Jacksonville, occurring in 1904 when she was 13, came under tragic circumstances. Just two weeks after her mother's death, Hurston's father shipped her off to boarding school. As she later wrote, "that hour began my wanderings."

Hurston spent the next decade living with siblings and working menial jobs around Jacksonville and elsewhere. Among her Jacksonville residences was her brother John Cornelius Hurston's house on Evergreen Avenue, where she lived from 1914 to 1915. Subsequently, Hurston resumed her education and launched her writing career. In 1925, she moved to New York, where she studied anthropology and became a leading light in the Harlem Renaissance, meeting James Weldon Johnson (see page 22). Among her published works was a landmark folklore collection, *Mules and Men*, and two novels, including her 1937 masterpiece *Their Eyes Were Watching God*.

In 1939, Hurston was back in Jacksonville working for the Federal Writers Project. Stetson Kennedy (see page 176) was her supervisor, and her office was at the Clara White Mission (see page 26). In 1942, she lived in St. Augustine, where she taught at Florida Normal and

In addition to Hurston, the DuPont Center mural depicts five other Black writers, educators, and civil rights leaders from Jacksonville. It was created in 2020 by artist Celso Gonzalez.

Top: *Zora Neale Hurston mosaic in Downtown Jacksonville.* Inset: *The John Cornelius Hurston House, where Zora lived and visited.*

JOHN CORNELIUS HURSTON HOUSE

WHAT: Former residence of Zora Neale Hurston

WHERE: 1473 Evergreen Ave.

COST: Free

PRO TIP: Read Hurston's *Their Eyes Were Watching God* and *Dust Tracks on a Road* for a depiction of Jacksonville in the early 20th century.

Industrial College (later Florida Memorial College) and completed her autobiography, *Dust Tracks on a Road*.

Hurston's dialect-heavy writing fell out of favor toward the end of her life, and she died in relative obscurity in 1960. A reappraisal of her work since the 1970s has restored her place in American literature and history. Today, a historical plaque marks her former St. Augustine home, and Jacksonville celebrates her in a mural at the Jessie Ball DuPont Center.

BIG JIM

What's that noise you hear across Downtown four times a day?

Big Jim is a Jacksonville icon that's seldom seen but is heard every day by people across Springfield, Downtown, and beyond. Known as the "oldest city employee," Jim is a massive steam whistle atop the JEA water plant whose blasts ring out four times a day and can be heard for miles.

Big Jim was designed in 1890 by John Einig, a marine engineer at the S. B. Hubbard Company. In his spare time, Einig designed steam whistles and hoped to invent the world's biggest. For Big Jim, Einig drafted the design and enlisted his brother-in-law Jim Patterson to fabricate it. As thanks, Einig named the whistle after Patterson.

Big Jim was so large that the only local facility that produced enough steam to blow it was the city waterworks. Built starting in 1879, the waterworks are historic in their own right. In 1887, they hosted the Sub-Tropical Exposition with guests that included President Grover Cleveland. City officials

BIG JIM

WHAT: A massive steam whistle in service since 1890

WHERE: 1002 N Main St.

COST: Free

PRO TIP: Springfield's Klutho Park is a great place to hear Big Jim.

The Springfield waterworks still work. JEA uses it as a water quality testing lab.

Big Jim atop the JEA waterworks

granted Einig use of the waterworks boilers to test Big Jim, and listeners were almost literally blown away by the results. The city was so impressed they asked Einig to leave the whistle in place permanently. Jim remained there until 1966, when it was moved to the Southside Generating Station on Downtown's Southbank. When JEA closed the generating station in 2001, they moved Big Jim back to the waterworks. By then, the waterworks no longer boiled water for steam, so JEA brought in special equipment to power Big Jim.

Big Jim typically sounds off at 7 a.m., 12 p.m., 1 p.m., and 5 p.m. It has fallen silent a few times over the years from mechanical failures and lightning strikes, each time drawing calls from worried citizens, but without fail, the oldest city employee has always returned to duty.

KARPELES MANUSCRIPT LIBRARY MUSEUM

How did a former church become a repository for the world's largest private manuscript collection?

Most museums rely on historical documents to create their exhibits. At the Karpeles Manuscript Library Museum, historical documents are the exhibits. A true hidden First Coast treasure, the classical revival building on 1st Street in Springfield plays host to the largest private collection of important manuscripts in the world.

How is that possible? The Jacksonville museum is in fact one of several across the country owned by David and Marsha Karpeles to house their overwhelming collection. David Karpeles, a math professor from Santa Barbara, California, who'd made a fortune in real estate, became interested in manuscripts in the 1970s. Learning that many significant manuscripts were in private collections, he decided to start a collection of his own. In 1978, he made his first purchase, a copy of the Emancipation Proclamation with Abraham Lincoln's signature, and was immediately hooked. He bought manuscripts at such a rate that prices skyrocketed. By 2000, his collection had grown to more than 1 million documents, the single largest collection in the world.

In the 1980s, Karpeles began looking for options to store his collection and to share it with others. The solution was a group of museums mostly in midsized cities across the country. In Jacksonville, his daughter and son-in-law located a building that

As of 2021, the Jacksonville museum is now one of 17 where David Karpeles displays his collection.

Karpeles Manuscript Library Museum

seemed like a perfect fit. Built in 1921 for the First Church of Christ, Scientist, Jacksonville's oldest Christian Scientist congregation, the imposing building was a contributing structure in the Springfield Historic District. The congregation had declined, and the church was looking to sell. Karpeles bought the church, and the Jacksonville branch of his museum opened in 1992. Since that time, the museum has displayed items from the Karpeles collection as well as art and manuscripts from other collectors, with four themed exhibits a year, all free to anyone who wants a look at significant documents from history.

KARPELES MANUSCRIPT LIBRARY MUSEUM

WHAT: Museum housing the world's largest manuscript collection

WHERE: 101 W 1st St.

COST: Free

PRO TIP: The Karpeles Museum hosts regular events and gallery openings that are always worth checking out.

GARLIC CRABS

What's a "Jacksonville-style" garlic crab?

While folks from New Orleans prefer Zatarain's and Baltimoreans go for Old Bay, Jaxsons like their crabs cooked in garlic butter. While garlic crabs can be had across the coastal South, Jacksonville is the world capital of the dish, which can be found at dozens of local crab shacks and restaurants primarily in Northside neighborhoods.

Garlic crabs are a variant of the well-known seafood boil. The crabs are cooked in a garlic butter sauce with sausage, corn, eggs, and potatoes. Native blue crabs are traditional, but snow crabs or garlic shrimp will do. Like the seafood boil, garlic crabs are among the many Southern dishes that originate with the Gullah Geechee people (see page 148). The Gullah Geechee descended from West Africans enslaved in the Lowcountry, the coastal region stretching from North Carolina to St. Augustine. On Lowcountry plantations, the Gullah Geechee maintained their own culture, including a distinctive cuisine that adapted their ancestors' culinary traditions using locally available ingredients. Like many Gullah Geechee recipes, garlic crabs use proteins from the local environment mixed with other common staples and flavorful spices to make a delicious, wholesome meal that could feed the whole family. Other dishes of Gullah Geechee origin include shrimp and grits, Hoppin' John, salmon patties, and she-crab soup.

GARLIC CRABS

WHAT: A Gullah Geechee dish of blue crabs boiled in garlic butter sauce

WHERE: All over Northeast Florida, especially Jacksonville's Northside

COST: Varies

PRO TIP: Garlic shrimp made with local Mayport shrimp are another Jacksonville delicacy.

Zebo's Crab Shack, one of Jacksonville's many garlic crab joints

Being the place with the largest population of Gullah Geechee descendants in the US, Jacksonville probably has more garlic crab joints than any other city. Garlic crabs are another thing Jacksonville doesn't give itself enough credit for, but nonetheless some folks travel to the city from far and wide for them, and in other cities, the dish sometimes appears on menus as Jacksonville-style garlic crabs. Hopefully, more Jaxsons will come to appreciate them as a pure Duval delicacy.

Traditionally, blue crabs were caught with a chicken bone on a fishing line, but today crab traps are more common.

EVERGREEN CEMETERY: HISTORY WRITTEN ON THE TOMBSTONES

Where can you find the graves of many of Jacksonville's influential people?

I'm fond of an old saying: the history of a city is written upon its tombstones. You can often learn more about a place from its cemeteries than from its main attractions and hot spots. In Jacksonville, Evergreen Cemetery, the city's oldest burial place still in active use, offers a record of 14 decades of life in the River City.

Jacksonville's earlier cemeteries, including Old City Cemetery (see page 32), were located in urban areas. As part of the rural cemeteries movement, which sought out more expansive spaces outside the city, Evergreen Cemetery opened in a then-remote area north of Jacksonville. Its founders hoped to create a necropolis, or city of the dead, where anyone from Jacksonville

---

EVERGREEN CEMETERY

WHAT: Jacksonville's oldest cemetery still in active operation

WHERE: 4535 N Main St.

COST: Free

PRO TIP: Evergreen Cemetery is huge. Ask the cemetery managers for a map.

One of Evergreen Cemetery's most striking features is its 96-foot-tall carillon tower, built in 1978 and featuring Westminster chimes and horns.

Left: *The Bellman Carillon Tower at Evergreen Cemetery.* Inset: *Grave of Isaiah D. Hart and family.*

could be buried. Its 180 acres included sections for African Americans, Catholics, several Jewish congregations, and social groups, including the Freemasons and Woodmen of the World. It contains the graves of 14 Jacksonville mayors, five governors of Florida, four US senators, and numerous other political and social leaders, as well as thousands of everyday Jaxsons of all ethnicities and backgrounds.

Among the buried is Isaiah D. Hart, the founder of Jacksonville, and members of the Hart family, including his son, Florida governor Ossian Hart. Also among the buried is Cora Crane, a Jacksonville brothel owner who married author Stephen Crane and launched her own writing career. Others include suffragists Mary Nolan and Grace Wilbur Trout, three passengers on the Titanic, and the Cummer family, founders of the Cummer Museum. Evergreen features Jacksonville's first Civil War monument, standing over the graves of Union servicemen. Erected in 1891, the Union monument predated the several Confederate monuments once found in the city. Featuring intricate headstones, stately mausoleums, and hundreds of trees, Evergreen is worth a visit for anyone interested in history, architecture, or simply a quiet walk.

THOMPSON WILLIAMS'S GRAVE—A PAINFUL SECRET

Why is there a headstone in the middle of a Durkeeville sidewalk?

A gravestone in the middle of a sidewalk by Durkeeville's Emmett Reed Park is a reminder of two tragedies: one of a life cut short, the other of a Black cemetery erased.

On the evening of October 28, 1908, Thompson Williams, a Black stevedore from the Eastside neighborhood of Fisher's Corner, heard screams. Running to help, he found his White neighbor, May Kooker, being assaulted. The assailant ran, but shot Williams as he fled. Williams died two days later at 51, leaving behind wife Candice and 10 children. No one was ever charged with his killing.

Local press hailed Williams as a hero for saving a White woman, and the *Jacksonville Metropolis* established a fund to erect a memorial and support his family. Many White citizens and several prominent Black citizens chipped in, ultimately raising $135.50. The fund commissioned a sizable headstone, bearing this inscription: "This tablet marks the grave of Thompson Williams, a Negro who died on October 28, 1908 from wounds received while endeavoring to protect the honor and life of a white woman."

THOMPSON WILLIAMS GRAVE AT EMMETT REED PARK

WHAT: A lone grave standing in the middle of the sidewalk by Emmett Reed Park

WHERE: Outside the Emmett Reed Community Center at 1093 W Sixth St.

COST: Free

PRO TIP: Williams's grave isn't the only one still remaining at Emmett Reed Park. The Fagins family plot can be seen in a wooded part of the park.

The headstone and grave in the middle of the sidewalk

Williams was buried in Mount Herman Cemetery, then a prominent burial place for Black citizens. By 1941, Mount Herman had fallen into disarray, and the owners deeded it to the city on the condition that it be maintained as a cemetery or park. In 1953, the city initiated plans to redevelop it as a park, in order to replace an older African American park paved over for I-95. Some graves and headstones were moved, but many more were left beneath the new Emmett Reed Park, which opened in 1969.

The city left Williams's grave in place, running the sidewalk around it. It stands as a reminder not only of Williams, but of a historic Black cemetery that, like too many others, has been nearly erased from existence.

Emmett Reed Park is named for the first Black employee of Jacksonville's parks department. A popular neighborhood park serving Durkeeville, it features a community center, pool, tennis courts, and more.

EDWARD WATERS UNIVERSITY, FLORIDA'S OLDEST HBCU

Where is Jacksonville's oldest higher educational institution?

Located on Kings Avenue, Edward Waters University is the oldest historically Black college in Florida and one of the oldest anywhere. Dating back to 1866, it's also the oldest private educational institution in the state and the only surviving historic college in Jacksonville's Urban Core.

Edward Waters started out as the Brown Theological Institute, founded in Live Oak by Bishop Charles H. Pearce, the founder of the African Methodist Episcopal (AME) Church in Florida. The institute's purpose was to educate the formerly enslaved, with a particular focus on preparing students to be AME ministers.

After facing storm damage and financial trouble, the college relocated to the basement of Jacksonville's Mount Zion AME Church. The school was reorganized as the East Florida Conference Divinity High School, and new facilities were built in Downtown Jacksonville. In 1892, the school graduated its first class in Jacksonville and was renamed Edward Waters College, after the third bishop of the AME Church.

Like most of Downtown Jacksonville, Edward Waters was destroyed by the Great Fire of 1901 (see page 2). In 1904, the college bought its current property off Kings Avenue, then a mostly rural area. Over the next few years, several primarily African American

---

EDWARD WATERS UNIVERSITY

WHAT: Florida's oldest historically Black university

WHERE: 1658 Kings Rd.

COST: Free

PRO TIP: Catch an Edward Waters Tigers baseball game at historic J. P. Small Park (page 50).

Centennial Hall at Edward Waters University

neighborhoods, including College Gardens, New Town, and Durkeeville, grew up around the campus. Changes continued for the college; in 1955, its two-year degree programs received regional accreditation, and it once again became a four-year college in 1979. In 2021, the school introduced graduate classes and changed its name to Edward Waters University.

Edward Waters survived as other local colleges failed or relocated to the suburbs, and today it is Jacksonville's only remaining college located entirely within the Urban Core. Featuring an attractive, walkable campus and various unique buildings, it's in the heart of Jacksonville's Mid-Westside.

Built in 1916, Centennial Hall is the oldest building at Edward Waters and home to the Obi-Scott-Umunna Collection of African art.

J. P. SMALL PARK—HOME OF FLORIDA'S FIRST MAJOR LEAGUERS

Where did Florida's only Negro Major League baseball team play?

Originally known as Barrs Field and then as Durkee Field, Henry L. Aaron Field at J. P. Small Memorial Stadium is Jacksonville's oldest surviving sports stadium. Established in the primarily Black neighborhood of Durkeeville in 1912, it hosted Jacksonville's earliest minor league baseball teams, major league spring training, and even the first Florida-Georgia football game both teams recognize.

The city purchased the stadium in 1926 and renovated it extensively in 1936. In 1938, it made history as home to the Jacksonville Red Caps of the Negro American League (NAL), the only Negro Major League team in Florida history. At a time when Major League Baseball (MLB) barred African Americans, the Negro Majors boasted equivalent talent. The Red Caps were organized by the Jacksonville Union Terminal, and the players were all railroad porters whose red hats were the source of the team's name. The Red Caps became the Cleveland Bears between 1939 and 1940 before returning to Jacksonville from 1941 to 1942, after which they departed the NAL. Today, MLB recognizes the Negro Majors as major league teams, making the Red Caps Florida's first major league team in any sport.

Another defining moment in Jacksonville sports occurred at Durkee Field in 1953. Samuel Wolfson, owner of the minor league Jacksonville Braves, broke the city's baseball color line by signing three Black players: Hank Aaron, Felix Mantilla, and Horace Garner. One of the first integrated teams in the South, the 1953 Braves were a smashing success, drawing huge crowds and becoming the league's regular-season champions.

Right: *J. P. Small Memorial Stadium.* Inset: *Jacksonville Red Caps jersey.*

HENRY L. AARON FIELD AT J. P. SMALL MEMORIAL STADIUM

WHAT: Jacksonville's only remaining historic baseball stadium

WHERE: 1701 Myrtle Ave. N

COST: Free

PRO TIP: To visit the baseball museum at the stadium, contact the Durkeeville Historical Society at durkeevillehistoricalsociety.org.

The stadium was left in place when the Braves moved to the new Wolfson Park in 1954. It serves as the home stadium for the Stanton College Prep and Edward Waters University (see page 48) baseball teams. In recognition of its importance to Jacksonville's African American and sports history, the stadium has undergone renovations, including the addition of a small museum of Jacksonville baseball.

The Jacksonville Jumbo Shrimp and Tampa Bay Rays have worn Red Caps throwback uniforms to celebrate Florida's first major league team.

HOLLEY'S BAR B Q

Were curly fries invented at Jacksonville's oldest barbecue joint?

Though unknown to much of the city, Jacksonville's oldest and longest continually operating barbecue joint—and possibly its oldest eatery of any kind—can be found in an unassuming block building on Moncrief Road. Founded in 1937 by Jack Holley, this small but exquisite hole-in-the-wall has been a family affair for more than 80 years.

Barbecue has a very long history in Jacksonville. The native Mocama Timucua smoked meats and fish over an open flame, and the Spanish, who introduced the pig to the New World, learned the technique from the natives and spread it widely. The Jacksonville area is home to many renowned barbecue joints, but Holley's is the oldest.

Holley's is a strictly takeout business, with no seating or picnic tables. Though revered in the neighborhood for its meats, it has another claim to fame: it is said to be the birthplace of curly fries. According to Wendy Holley, owner of

---

HOLLEY'S BAR B Q

WHAT: Jacksonville's oldest barbecue joint

WHERE: 3604 Moncrief Rd.

COST: The cost of a great plate of barbecue

PRO TIP: Thirsty? Order a honey dripper, a local frozen treat.

Jacksonville is home to a lot of delicious barbecue. Other old school joints to try include Fred Cotten's Landmark BBQ, Jenkins Quality Barbecue, and Lou Bono Bar-B-Q.

Holley's Bar B Q

the restaurant and daughter of founder Jack Holley, her father invented curly fries in the early days of the business, and even had his brother Leroy Holley build a machine to cut potatoes into curls. She believes he could have had a patent on curly fries, but because he couldn't read or write, he was swindled out of the credit. Other restaurants also claim to have invented curly fries, including Oklahoma City's Dolores Restaurant & Drive In, which claims to have served "Suzie-Q fries" as early as 1938. But regardless, Holley's curly fries are legit.

Holley's is a secret to much of Jacksonville largely due to the neighborhood it serves, which many locals consider dangerous. But for those willing to venture out, the food and history are well worth the trip.

MONCRIEF SPRINGS AND WHITE HARVEST FARMS

Is a secret French treasure hidden in a lost Northwest Jacksonville spring?

Moncrief Creek has one of Jacksonville's most mysterious place-names. It appears as "Mountchief" or "Mountcrief" on early 19th-century maps, but it's unclear where the names came from. One 1874 promotional account offers an explanation, and it's a doozy.

The story goes that pawnbroker Eugene Moncrief escaped the French Revolution with nine chests of riches. Entering the St. Johns River, he buried eight chests somewhere at Moncrief Creek's springhead, and he used the ninth to court a Native American woman named Sunflower. Moncrief was soon murdered by Sunflower's paramour, Great Powder, but the conspirators died in a canoe accident before recovering the treasure, which still lay out there for the finding. The context is that in 1874, former Jacksonville mayor Peter Jones purchased Moncrief Springs to establish a resort featuring swimming, bowling, a racetrack, and other amenities. The promotional (and implausible) nature of the account suggests the story is hokum, but it did the trick, as the resort remained popular until Florida outlawed horse racing in 1911.

In 1945, when the area around the springs had been developed as a predominantly Black neighborhood, Clara White Mission founder Eartha White (see page 26) purchased the old resort to redevelop

(see page 26)

> ## WHITE HARVEST FARMS
>
> **WHAT:** Urban farm on the site of the former Moncrief Springs
>
> **WHERE:** 5232–5298 Moncrief Rd.
>
> **COST:** Free
>
> **PRO TIP:** Visit the farmers market from 10 a.m. to 2 p.m. each Saturday from October to June.

Columns at White Harvest Farms dating to the property's days as a swimming resort

as a boys club and swimming pool for African Americans excluded at every other pool in the city. This had closed by 1963, by which time the springs themselves had been lost under development.

Just as Eartha White once transformed the abandoned original resort, the Clara White Mission found a way to reinvent the property to benefit the community. In 2012, the organization turned the site into White Harvest Farms, an urban farm growing healthy food for Northwest Jacksonville. It has been continuously expanded ever since, and now has its own farmers market and job-training facility. It seems there's treasure in the land after all.

Three Corinthian columns, now painted with the name of White Harvest Farms, are among the few physical reminders of the farm's resort past.

FLORIDA NATIVE BIRD ROOKERY AT THE JACKSONVILLE ZOO

How did the Jacksonville zoo become a haven for local wildlife?

Since 1914, the Jacksonville Zoo and Gardens has been a popular regional institution. Occupying 122 acres along the Trout River, its enclosures are home to more than 2,000 animals from around the world, including award-winning exhibits for tigers, jaguars, gorillas, giant otters, bonobos, and more. Less known is the fact that the zoo is also one of the best, most accessible places to see indigenous wildlife in North Florida.

The Jacksonville Zoo's efforts to create a safe and comfortable environment for its residents also make it ideal for many wild birds and animals. While uninvited wild guests have always been at the zoo, in 1999, one group put the institution at the forefront of a push for zoos to embrace and provide safe places for native species. A flock of 14 wood storks, displaced by habitat destruction, settled in the live oaks of the Africa Loop, overlooking the antelopes and rhinos. These large storks are a threatened species in the US, with American breeding populations restricted to Florida, Georgia, and South Carolina. The zoo embraced the newcomers, launching

The Jacksonville Zoo also has the Wild Florida section, a more traditional exhibit featuring native species such as Florida panthers, black bears, and alligators.

Wood storks nesting at the Jacksonville Zoo. Photo by Stephanie Morse

a conservation and monitoring project in 2003. The population grew into a thriving breeding colony; with a population of several hundred, it is now one of the largest wood stork rookeries in the US and probably the most visible.

Many other species can be seen on the zoo grounds. A massive colony of night herons roosts above the cheetah enclosure. Other birds visitors may see on any given day include green herons, seagulls, anhingas, roseate spoonbills, and many songbirds. Manatees are also a common sight at the zoo's Trout River dock. In 2017, the zoo committed to protecting these endangered natives with Northeast Florida's first manatee critical care center, where sick or injured manatees are nursed back to health and released back into the wild.

NATIVE BIRD ROOKERIES AT JACKSONVILLE ZOO

WHAT: Wild natives making the zoo their home

WHERE: 370 Zoo Pkwy.

COST: Standard tickets are $24.95 for adults and teens, $19.95 for kids 3–12, and $22.95 for seniors.

PRO TIP: Some birders come to the zoo hours before it opens to spot birds in the outer areas and ponds.

DEVIL'S SCHOOL: HAUNTED ANNIE LYTLE ELEMENTARY

What's inside Jacksonville's most haunted place?

Annie Lytle Elementary School, also known as Public School Number 4, has long had a reputation as the "most haunted place in Jacksonville." The imposing neoclassical building is certainly fertile territory for ghost stories. It opened in 1917 as an elementary school serving White students in rapidly growing Riverside. In 1950, it was renamed in honor of longtime principal Annie Lytle Housh.

By then, the community had begun to outgrow the aging school. Additionally, when the interstates and the original Fuller Warren Bridge were constructed in the 1950s, they cut the school off from its neighborhood. It closed in 1960 and served increasingly sporadically as administrative offices until 1981.

When remodeling plans fell apart, the building shuttered for good. However, being both spooky looking and highly visible— it's easily seen from the highway—it soon entered local folklore. It emerged as Jacksonville's most popular mecca for legend tripping, the rite of passage in which young adults prove (or at least scare) themselves by venturing to frightening locations.

As all good legend-tripping destinations need a scary story to set the tone, Annie Lytle Elementary acquired several especially memorable, if totally specious, legends. Most commonly, the

Annie Lytle Elementary is just one of several local sites that have become popular for legend tripping in recent decades. Others include Ghost Light Road (page 178) and the Wiccademous grave (page 114).

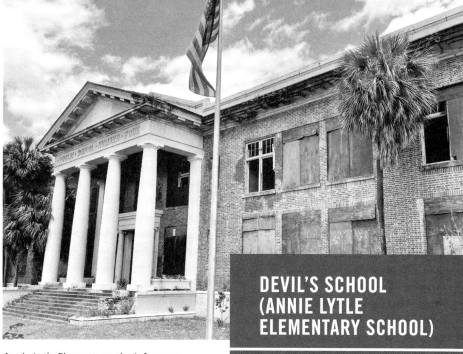

Annie Lytle Elementary, the infamous "Devil's School"

DEVIL'S SCHOOL (ANNIE LYTLE ELEMENTARY SCHOOL)

WHAT: A former public school that became the city's predominate legend-tripping destination

WHERE: The corner of Peninsular Place and Chelsea Street

COST: Free

PRO TIP: Trespassing laws are strictly enforced at Annie Lytle Elementary, so don't enter without express permission.

school is said to be haunted by schoolchildren killed in a boiler explosion or, more outrageously, by a murderous janitor or cannibal principal. Inspired by contemporary hysteria over satanic cults, the school also came to be seen as a site of devil worship, earning the nickname "Devil's School."

Unfortunately, all this attention has taken a toll on the school. It was routinely vandalized and suffered several fires; nearly every wall was covered with graffiti. Finally, local preservationists worked with neighborhood groups and police to protect the school from further intrusion. While a restoration plan remains elusive, the building is now stable as it awaits whatever the future holds.

SUN-RAY CINEMA

What's the best place to see a movie in Jacksonville?

Jacksonville's coolest movie theater is also one of its most historically significant. What's now known as Sun-Ray Cinema is the city's oldest surviving movie theater, although it hasn't been open continuously. It was also the first theater in Florida to show "talkies," or sound films. Today, it's a place where you can watch an art house movie over a cold craft beer, a vegan sandwich, and some of the best pizza in the First Coast.

Originally named the Riverside Theater and later the 5 Points Theater, it opened in March 1927 in a new five-story Renaissance revival-style building. At the time, Riverside was a booming streetcar suburb southwest of Downtown Jacksonville, and Five Points was emerging as its neighborhood commercial district. The building included additional commercial space and offices on the higher floors. The first theater in Florida and third in the country equipped with a Vitaphone to show sound films, it attracted national attention for screening *Don Juan*, the first feature film with synchronized sound. The theater and building were renovated in 1949, adding the marquee still in place today.

The aging theater declined in the 1970s and shut down in the early 1980s. It later served as a performance theater, and from 1991 to 2004, it was home to Club Five, a nightclub that used the stage for music and shows. In 2004, it reopened as a movie theater, and new owners Shana David-Massett and Tim Massett undertook an

---

The theater's original architect was Roy Benjamin, who also helped create Downtown's Florida Theatre and San Marco Theatre, open in San Marco Square since 1938.

Sun-Ray Cinema

SUN-RAY CINEMA

WHAT: Artsy, historic movie theater

WHERE: 1028 Park St.

COST: About $10 for movie tickets

PRO TIP: Check out the mural of the *Creature from the Black Lagoon*, a movie with local ties (see page 190).

extensive remodeling in 2011 to add a new screen, seats, and equipment. Renamed Sun-Ray Cinema, it is known across the First Coast as the best place to catch art house, foreign, and independent movies other theaters often don't show, though it screens the blockbusters as well. Sun-Ray has continued to expand, adding a second theater and an attached restaurant, the Pizza Cave, which purveys their famous pies in a cavernously decorated storefront.

JIFFY FEET DON'T FAIL ME NOW

How did a slang term for dirty feet become a Jacksonville icon?

"Jiffy feet" is a colloquialism for bare feet blackened by dirt and asphalt—as when one forgoes shoes during a convenience store run—that's pervasive across the First Coast. In fact, it's so well known that Jaxsons often don't realize it's specific to this area and largely unknown elsewhere.

The phrase has unusual origins. It comes from the long-gone Orange Park–based convenience store chain Huntley Jiffy (or simply Jiffy), which once had 342 stores across northern Florida and southern Georgia. Existing from 1965 until the chain was bought out in 1990, the stores were once so omnipresent in the Jacksonville area that "Jiffy" became a local generic term for convenience stores.

JIFFY FEET

WHAT: Jacksonville area colloquialism for dirty bare feet

WHERE: They're everywhere, but check out the installation of R. Land Jiffies at Birdie's in Riverside: 1044 Park St.

COST: Free

PRO TIP: Jacksonville pavement gets incredibly hot, so build up those calluses before trying for your own Jiffy feet.

The term "Jiffy feet," as in the dirty feet you'd get walking to the Jiffy without shoes, apparently emerged in the 1970s. It became the Jacksonville version of similar terms such as "K-Mart feet," "grocery store feet," and "gypsy feet," and was widespread by the 1980s. The phrase outlived the chain that inspired it, to the point that many younger Jaxsons have no idea of its origins.

Jiffy feet got a substantial boost in popularity in the 21st century thanks to a particularly memorable art project. Atlanta-based artist R. Land grew up on Jacksonville's Northside in the 1980s, and the locale inspires much of his work. In 2008, while devising a Jacksonville street

Left: *Jiffy tree at Birdie's bar.* Right: *Two Jiffy feet by R. Land.*

art project, he returned to his memories of locals striding around with Jiffy feet. The result was a series of cartoony black-soled feet in Land's signature style, which were affixed to telephone poles across Riverside. The initial series was a hit, and Land was swamped with requests. Over the years, Land has designed hundreds of different Jiffy feet, ensuring the "Jiffy feet" phrase will stick around like so much tarmac on locals' soles.

Probably the best display of R. Land's Jiffy feet is the "Jiffy tree" at Birdie's bar in Riverside. It's just to the right of the bar.

WILLOWBRANCH PARK: JACKSONVILLE'S LGBTQ HOLY GROUND

How did this quiet Riverside park kick off LGBTQ rights in Jacksonville?

For decades, Willowbranch Park and the adjacent Willowbranch Library have held special significance to Jacksonville's LGBTQ community. At the center of Jacksonville's oldest "gayborhood," it's been the site of hushed meetings and boisterous celebrations. Some even call it "holy ground."

The park dates to 1916, when it became a new public space in an expanding part of Riverside. The Mediterranean Revival-style library opened in 1930 as the city's second branch library. Willowbranch Creek wends through the park before passing through a culvert under Park Street.

Formerly well-to-do Riverside saw its housing values drop as White flight and suburbanization set in the 1960s, and cheaper rent drew in a more bohemian element. The Allman Brothers Band grew out of public jams hosted at Willowbranch Park in 1969 (see page 64). Among the neighborhood's pioneers were Jacksonville's LGBTQ community. Jacksonville's first Gay Pride Festival was held at Willowbranch Park in 1978, nine years after the Stonewall Riots in New York galvanized the gay rights movement. Today, River City Pride is a massive celebration featuring a parade through Riverside and a week of revelry in Five Points.

The marquee event of River City Pride, the Pride Parade, usually begins at Willowbranch Park before winding through the neighborhood.

Top: *The mural at Willowbranch Park.*
Inset: *Willowbranch Library.*

WILLOWBRANCH PARK AND WILLOWBRANCH LIBRARY

WHAT: A city park in Riverside with a long and storied LGBTQ history

WHERE: 2870 Sydney St.

COST: Free

PRO TIP: Walk up the Willowbranch Creek to see the planted trees and mural.

Willowbranch Library has its own LGBTQ history. At a time of severe oppression, the library became a popular spot for LGBTQ Jaxsons to meet in relative safety. Local LGBTQ youth organization JASMYN, one of Jacksonville's most prominent LGBTQ nonprofits, formed at the library in 1991 when a group of young adults began meeting there for solidarity.

In the 2010s, organizers and the city launched a renovation of Willowbranch Park dedicated to its long LGBTQ history and to victims of AIDS. The Willowbranch Creek culvert has been painted with a mural, and the park is undergoing reforesting to create Love Grove. Advocates hope to add public artwork that would be Florida's second AIDS memorial.

CAMEL RIDERS: DELICIOUSNESS IN A PITA

What is Jacksonville's signature sandwich?

Camel riders are Jacksonville's most distinctive local food product—our answer to the Philly cheesesteak, Nashville hot chicken, or Rochester's garbage plate. Traditional camel riders comprise a pita stuffed with ham, salami, bologna, and sandwich fixings, and they have been part of Jacksonville's culinary fabric since the 1960s. While riders can be found in some other cities, only Jacksonville can boast them in concentration.

Camel riders and other rider variations are a product of Jacksonville's large and vibrant Arab American community. Arab immigrants came to Jacksonville starting in the 1890s, and ever since, the community has been influential in all parts of life, from politics to health care to business. One area where Arab Americans have been especially prevalent is the restaurant industry. Nearly every neighborhood has its own Arab-owned deli, restaurant, shop, or bar, and many have riders on the menu.

The camel rider's origin is often traced to Joe Assi, a Lebanese-born baker. In the early 1960s, he owned the Gold Room restaurant, where he started selling a cold-cut sandwich he ultimately named the "desert rider." Some other restaurateurs doubt this story, but regardless, the unpretentious "Arab club sandwich" took off as a cheap, tasty meal for working folks on the go. By the mid-1970s, riders had spread across Jacksonville at eateries such as the Sheik,

The steak-in-a-sack, featuring steak and onions in a pita, is nearly as old as the traditional camel rider.

A traditional camel rider from Pinegrove Market and Deli

WHAT: A cold-cut sandwich in a pita

WHERE: Dozens of restaurants and sandwich shops across town

COST: About $5

PRO TIP: My favorite camel riders come from Pinegrove Market and Deli in Avondale.

Desert Rider, and Pinegrove Market & Deli; today more than 50 restaurants serve them. Since 1978, Joe Assi's nephew Melad Assi has operated the Pita Bakery in Arlington, which supplies many local restaurants.

Some restaurateurs avoid the "camel rider" name as culturally insensitive. Different varieties of riders have become common, including the steak-in-a-sack, veggie rider, and shrimp rider. Under any name and construction, riders are a true Jacksonville staple and one of the many legacies of the city's Arab American community.

GRAY HOUSE: BIRTHPLACE OF THE ALLMAN BROTHERS BAND, SOUTHERN ROCK PIONEERS

Where did the first great Southern rock band get their start?

March 23, 1969 has a place in American music history as the day of "The Jam," in which the legendary Southern rock group the Allman Brothers Band came to be. The old Victorian home at 2844 Riverside Ave. where it happened is known in rock lore as the Gray House.

The Gray House was built in 1912 in the eclectic Riverside neighborhood. In 1969, it was home to bassist Berry Oakley and guitarist Dickie Betts, future Allman Brothers members. Guitarist Duane Allman often crashed there as well when he was in town. Riverside had become a bohemian enclave in the 1960s as dropping housing prices brought in throngs of musicians, artists, and hippies. Taking advantage of the energy, Allman and company routinely joined other musicians to jam at Willowbranch Park (see page 64) and local bars.

Allman had a concept for a new, bluesy band featuring two guitarists and two drummers, and on March 23, he invited Oakley, Betts, keyboardist Reese Wynans, and drummers Johnny "Jaimoe" Johnson and Butch Trucks for a session at the Gray House. The Jam

Gregg Allman wrote the legendary song "Whipping Post" while at the Gray House. Not having a pen or paper, he wrote the lyrics on an ironing board cover with burnt matches.

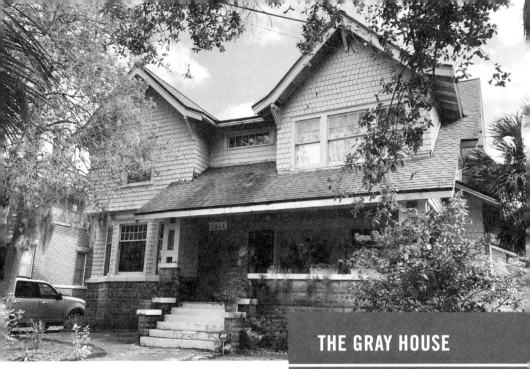

The Gray House, birthplace of the Allman Brothers Band

THE GRAY HOUSE

WHAT: The house where the Allman Brothers Band, the first prominent Southern rock group, was formed

WHERE: 2844 Riverside Ave.

COST: Free (historical marker is accessible from the sidewalk)

PRO TIP: Also check out the Green House at 2799 Riverside Ave. Berry Oakley and Dickie Betts lived there with their previous band, the Second Coming, before moving to the Gray House.

was so incendiary that Allman threatened to fight any of the musicians who tried to leave before agreeing to start a band. They still needed a singer, so Allman called his brother Gregg in LA. Gregg arrived three days later, and the original lineup of the Allman Brothers Band was set.

Although the band left Jacksonville for Macon, Georgia just weeks later, their influence locally was tremendous. Within the next few years, Jacksonville exploded as the epicenter of Southern rock, producing a string of successful bands such as Lynyrd Skynyrd, Cowboy, 38 Special, Molly Hatchet, and Blackfoot. The Gray House, where it all began, is now a private residence, owned by Dennis Price since 1986. Price and the state placed a historical marker out front in 2019.

ST. JOHNS RIVER MONSTER

Does a sea serpent inhabit the St. Johns River?

For decades, folks along the St. Johns River, from Jacksonville as far south as Kissimmee, have reported sightings of an immense sea creature, colloquially named "Johnnie," "Pinky," or "Borinkus." Though no one has ever gotten a photograph, Florida's answer to the Loch Ness Monster has been an enduring legend.

A newspaper story about a purported sea monster at the St. Johns River mouth in 1849 is often given as the earliest encounter, but it was not until the 1950s that sightings really took off. In 1953, Owen Godwin of Godwin's Snake Village in Kissimmee said a 30-foot serpent with a horn on its head was in the river, and he offered a reward for its capture.

Naturally, this led to a raft of sightings and newspaper reports across Central Florida. Scientists suggested that any authentic sightings were simply manatees, but retired State Attorney J. W. "Jesse" Hunter had a more entertaining explanation. He wrote to the paper that he'd seen many of the creatures, which he for some reason called "Borinkus," as far back as the 1910s, and that a Volusia citrus magnate even used a team of them to pull ferries.

In 1976, a group of friends reported seeing the monster in Jacksonville while fishing on a Southbank pier. They described the creature as a huge horned serpent the color of boiled shrimp; it was dubbed "Pinky." Residents subsequently came out of the woodwork to say they'd seen it too. Descriptions varied; some

The St. Johns Sea Monster is Jacksonville's most famous cryptid after the Bardin Booger (see page 140).

Wallace McLean's drawing of the St. Johns River Monster, from the Tampa Tribune, *January 18, 1976*

ST. JOHNS RIVER MONSTER

said it was gray, others black, and one said it had a split tail. Again, suggestions that the sightings could be manatees, eels, or a line of otters playing took a backseat to claims that it was definitely a monster. Sightings have continued sporadically ever since, so next time you visit the St. Johns, don't forget your phone.

WHAT: Legendary river serpent

WHERE: Anywhere on the St. Johns River. I recommend the Downtown Riverwalks, which have excellent views even if you don't see the monster.

COST: Free. In fact if you find it, many locals will buy you a beer.

PRO TIP: You may not see a monster, but you've got a good shot at seeing dolphins, manatees, and other creatures of the deep.

TREATY OAK— JACKSONVILLE'S OLDEST RESIDENT

Did a made-up legend save Jacksonville's oldest living thing?

This massive, gnarled old oak on the Southbank has accrued a number of legends over its approximately 250-year existence, many of which are entirely fictional. Fortunately, its real story is just as engrossing.

The tree's age has been debated for decades, but recent estimates put its birth around 1770, as the area was river marsh before that. It first achieved public prominence at the turn of the 20th century.

Originally called the Giant Oak, in 1907, it was made the centerpiece of Dixieland Park, an amusement park in the town of South Jacksonville (see also Marco Lake, page 76). The proprietors decked the great oak with electric lights and affixed a plaque that claimed, without evidence, that Seminole leader Osceola held councils there.

Dixieland Park declined as the US entered World War I in 1917, and the property was parceled out for development. By 1934, the Giant Oak itself was threatened with removal. To save it, *Florida Times-Union* reporter Pat Moran wrote an article on the tree's "history," elaborating on the Osceola story to claim that the Seminole and early settlers signed a treaty under its branches. Thus, it became known as the "Treaty Oak."

TREATY OAK

WHAT: An approximately 250-year-old live oak tree with a storied if largely fictional history

WHERE: Jessie Ball duPont Park, 1207 Prudential Dr.

COST: Free

PRO TIP: The park has several paths, boardwalks, and informational plaques worth checking out.

The Treaty Oak

Subsequently, philanthropist Jessie Ball duPont had her foundation purchase the Treaty Oak's lot to spare it. In 1964, the oak was threatened by a proposed apartment development on surrounding parcels, so duPont purchased those lots too. She transferred the whole property to the city for use as a park.

Today, Treaty Oak is 70 feet high and 145 feet wide, and its trunk is 25 feet in circumference. It is almost certainly the oldest living thing in Duval County and one of the oldest anywhere in Florida.

The Treaty Oak isn't the only Jacksonville tree saved by made-up stories. In 1942, Admiral Gilchrist B. Stockton used the same ruse to save the "Timucuan Oak" during the development of NAS Jacksonville (see page 130).

ST. JOHNS RIVER TAXI AND RIVER DOLPHINS

Yes, Jacksonville has river dolphins–but where can you see them?

The St. Johns River is Jacksonville's crown jewel, but sadly, options are fairly limited for interacting with it. Fortunately, the St. Johns River Taxi is there to fill some of the need with a daily taxi service and specialty tours.

ST. JOHNS RIVER TAXI

WHAT: A boat service with stops along the Northbank and Southbank Riverwalks and specialty cruises

WHERE: The main stop is at 1015 Museum Cir.

COST: $10 a day per person for the river taxi route; $18–$22 per person for tours

PRO TIP: You won't find a better date night than one of the taxi's sunset cruises.

Water taxis first came to Jacksonville in 1987 when the erstwhile Jacksonville Landing opened, giving Jacksonville a waterside marketplace for the first time in decades. Various taxi operators worked out of the Landing, ferrying pedestrians along stops on the Northbank and Southbank Riverwalks. The early days of Jacksonville water taxis were something of a riverine Wild West, with feuding captains swarming the docks during busy hours and being nowhere in sight the rest of the time.

To improve service, in 2002, the City Council shifted to a contract system where one operator was chosen to work a consistent schedule. Since 2015, this has been the St. Johns River Taxi. In addition to a daily route along the Riverwalks, they offer Saturday services to other neighborhoods and specialty cruises, including history tours and nighttime cruises.

For my money, their best specialty offering is the river dolphin tour. The St. Johns River is home to about 300 bottlenose dolphins.

Top: *River dolphins on the St. Johns.* Inset: *A dolphin cruise on the St. Johns River Taxi.*

The dolphins are a favorite sight for locals and visitors, but relatively little was known about them until 2011, when the University of North Florida launched the Dolphin Research Program to learn more about Jacksonville's urban cetaceans. The program discovered that about 150 dolphins are permanent year-round residents who never leave the river, which gives Jacksonville a distinction as one of the few North American cities to boast river dolphins. The playful cetaceans can often be seen from waterfront docks and parks, but the River Taxi provides the only dolphin-watching tour in town.

For more information on the river taxi stops, river dolphin tour, and other specialty tours, visit jaxrivertaxi.com.

MARCO LAKE

Who knew a former brickyard claypit could be so scenic?

Located just a block south of bustling San Marco Square is a picturesque space that's often missed even by folks in the neighborhood. A great spot for boating, fishing, and checking out fancy houses, Marco Lake is a manmade water feature with an unusual history.

The lake began as the claypit for the Gamble and Stockton Brickyard in the early 20th century. The brickyard was just south of the town of South Jacksonville, across the St. Johns River from Jacksonville. In the 1920s, the brickyard produced 50,000 bricks a day, providing material for homes built during the ill-fated Florida land boom.

In 1921, the St. Johns River Bridge opened, connecting Jacksonville and South Jacksonville by road. The brickyard's ownership, which included developer Telfair Stockton, sensed that their property would soon be more valuable as real estate. Stockton, who had developed the Avondale neighborhood in 1920, shuttered the brickyard and announced it would soon make way for a new neighborhood named San Marco after the famous Venice district. The project was such a success that when Jacksonville annexed South Jacksonville in 1930, locals came to know the former town as "San Marco."

Rather than fill in the old claypit, Stockton transformed it into a water feature. He installed a seawall and dug a canal out to the river to channel water in, and Marco

MARCO LAKE

WHAT: A half-mile long manmade water feature in the San Marco neighborhood

WHERE: The lake can be seen off Largo Road and from the Marco Lake Canal Bridge on River Road.

COST: Free

PRO TIP: Visit at dusk to see jumping whiting and spectacular sunsets over the water.

Marco Lake from above. Photo by Erik Hamilton

Lake was born. Within a few years, it was surrounded by new homes and tony mansions.

Marco Lake had no docks for boats for many years, and the canal was gated to prevent intrusion by invasive water hyacinths. Since the 1950s, however, many houses have added docks, and it became a popular destination in the neighborhood for boating and fishing. However, public access is limited to three small areas, so Marco Lake remains a secret even to many San Marco residents.

Marco Lake's not the only piece of the old brickyard still around. Up the street, an old artesian well was transformed into a fountain in Largo Well Park.

EL FARO MEMORIAL

What's the tragic story behind the monument under the Dames Point Bridge?

Hidden beneath the Dames Point Bridge is a memorial for one of the greatest tragedies in Jacksonville's long maritime history. On September 29, 2015, the cargo ship SS *El Faro* left Jacksonville for the last time. Bound for San Juan, Puerto Rico, on a routine voyage, the ship's crew comprised 33 mariners, about half of whom had Jacksonville ties. At the time, Tropical Storm Joaquin was brewing in the Caribbean, and the *El Faro*'s course would take it perilously close. Still, Captain Michael Davidson pressed on. On October 1, just off the Bahamas, the *El Faro* was battered by what was by that time Hurricane Joaquin. The crew abandoned ship as the *El Faro* took on water and sank. Sadly, rescue efforts were unsuccessful, and all 33 lives were lost.

As investigations and legal settlements commenced, the City of Jacksonville determined to establish a permanent monument to the lost. The city cleaned up a long-neglected space,

EL FARO MEMORIAL

WHAT: A memorial for the cargo ship *El Faro*, lost at sea in October 2015 along with 33 crew.

WHERE: Dames Point Park, at 9101 Dames Point Rd.

COST: Free

PRO TIP: The park is an excellent place to fish and see river dolphins.

Local legend holds that Dames Point is so called because local women waved to ships there. In reality, it's named for a former landowner, 18th-century sea captain Charles Dames.

Top: *33 mooring bollards dedicated to each lost crewmember.* Inset: *The* El Faro *memorial.*

Dames Point Park, as a home for the memorial. This park dates to 1988, during the construction of the Dames Point Bridge, but it was mostly inaccessible until the port extended the road to it in 2001.

Built in 2016, the *El Faro* memorial includes a 10-foot lighthouse statue (El Faro means "The Lighthouse" in Spanish) inscribed with the crewmembers' names. An identical companion statue stands in San Juan. Beside the Jacksonville memorial are 33 mooring bollards, one for each life lost.

The memorial's location has deep significance for Jacksonville, a major port city. Named for 18th-century sea captain Charles Dames, Dames Point is a prominent feature of the riverbank passed by ships calling on the Port of Jacksonville. With the addition of the *El Faro* memorial, Dames Point Park has become a moving if underknown place of remembrance for a sad chapter in Jacksonville's seafaring history.

KINGSLEY PLANTATION

How did an enslaved African princess become one of Florida's major planters?

One of Florida's most important historical sites, Kingsley Plantation, is the oldest surviving slave plantation in the state. It features a plantation house dating to 1797 and other buildings, including 23 small cocquina houses for the enslaved.

The plantation on Fort George Island dates to 1765. It went through several owners, the most famous being the Kingsleys, who ran it from 1814 until 1837. Zepheniah Kingsley and his wife Anna Madgigine Jai were perhaps the most unusual slaveholders in US history. Anna was a Wolof royal enslaved in present-day Senegal; Zepheniah purchased and married her around 1806, when she was 13. He later freed her, and she took an active role in managing his plantations. Their family included three other African wives and nine mixed-race children.

The Kingsleys were deeply invested in the Spanish system of slavery, which provided some rights for free and enslaved Africans. After the US takeover of Florida, increasingly repressive laws led the Kingsleys to leave for Haiti. The plantation passed through further owners, including the Ribault Club (see page 84). The state of Florida purchased the property as a park in 1955; it transferred to the National Parks Service in 1991 and became part of the Timucuan Ecological and Historic Preserve. While other preserved plantations typically focus on the slaveholders, Kingsley stands out by foregrounding the experiences of those enslaved on the land.

KINGSLEY PLANTATION

WHAT: Former slave plantation and historic site whose owners included Zepheniah and Anna Kingsley

WHERE: 11676 Palmetto Ave.

COST: Free

PRO TIP: Keep an eye out for peacocks, which live on the island.

Top: *Planter's house at Kingsley Plantation.* Bottom: *Homes of the enslaved. The one to the right has been restored to its 19th-century appearance.*

The Kingsley Plantation and the deep surrounding forest of moss-draped oaks loom large in local folklore. It's said to be haunted by a number of ghosts, most notoriously "Old Red Eyes," supposedly the spirit of a murderer lynched by his fellow enslaved, who now haunts the woods as a pair of glowing eyes. Such legends help connect people with the space, but this is one place where the history is more interesting than any ghost story.

Anna Kingsley and other family members later lived in a mixed-race community in Arlington. Kingsley died in 1870 and was buried in an unmarked grave in her family's cemetery there, Sammis Cemetery.

THE NEFF HOUSE AND THE MYSTERIOUS BETZ SPHERE

Will we ever know the truth about the strange metal orb found on Fort George Island?

In the woods of Fort George Island stands an unusual Tudor revival house. Built in 1927 by Mellen Clark Greeley, the "Dean of Jacksonville Architects," it features a unique entrance tower and balcony. It was built for Chicago businessman Nettleton Neff, but a series of tragedies prevented him from ever visiting. In 1926, Neff's wife died in a house fire, and, in 1928, their son committed suicide. In 1931, Neff took his own life.

The house's notoriety derives from a mystery that emerged decades later. In spring 1974, then-owners Gerri and Antoine Betz were walking in the woods with their son Terry when he came across something strange: a metallic sphere the size of a bowling ball. Terry took it home, and before long, said Gerri, it started displaying inexplicable properties: it hummed back when Terry played guitar, rolled around seemingly of its own volition, and emitted high-pitched sounds that set dogs whining.

Within weeks, the "Betz sphere" also known as the "mystery sphere," had drawn international press. Everyone wanted to know just what the thing was. An alien device? Top secret technology?

In 2019, WJCT Public Media released the excellent podcast "Odd Ball," the most comprehensive account of the Betz sphere to date. Check it out at wjct.org/podcasts/oddball.

Left: *The Neff House has seen better days.*
Inset: *Terry Betz with the sphere in 1974. Photo courtesy of the Jacksonville Public Library*

THE NEFF HOUSE

WHAT: A 1926 Tudor revival style home that was once home to the enigmatic "Betz sphere"

WHERE: The woods off Fort George Island Rd., near Kingsley Plantation Fort George Island

COST: Free

PRO TIP: While on Fort George Island, stop by some of the other attractions, including the Ribault Club (page 84) and Kingsley Plantation (page 80).

A simple check valve stopper from a paper mill? Theories and speculation abounded. Naval Station Mayport investigated but concluded only that it wasn't government property and was probably manmade. Next, a panel of UFO researchers, including Allen Hynek, the most famous ufologist of the period, examined it. They also failed to crack the mystery.

Eventually, the Betz family tired of the attention and simply stopped talking about the sphere. They sold their house in 1985, and the Florida Park Service took over in 1989. Researchers believe the family still has the orb, but nothing new has emerged. The Betz sphere still appears routinely in books, shows, and websites about unexplained phenomena, but for now, it remains a Jacksonville mystery.

MISSION SAN JUAN DEL PUERTO

Where was the Spanish mission to the local Native Americans?

Centuries before Jacksonville was founded, the region was home to the Timucua people. Fort George Island was once home to Alicamani, a political and cultural center of the Timucua group known as the Mocama, from the Timucua word for "ocean."

The Mocama inhabited coastal inlets and barrier islands from Cumberland Island in Georgia (see page 120) to present-day St. Augustine. When European contact began in 1562, the Mocama were divided into two chiefdoms: Tacatacuru on Cumberland Island and Saturiwa around the St. Johns River mouth. The Saturiwa, led by a chief also known as Saturiwa, comprised about 30 towns, including Alicamani.

The Saturiwa had mostly amiable relations with the French of Fort Caroline (page 16) in 1564 and 1565. When the Spanish established St. Augustine in 1565 and ejected the French, the Saturiwa led a coalition of resistance. Chief Saturiwa died

---

RIBAULT CLUB AND MISSION SAN JUAN DEL PUERTO MARKER

WHAT: Museum and historic marker

WHERE: 11241 Fort George Rd.

COST: Free

PRO TIP: Launch a kayak from the Ribault Club for a different view of the island.

The Ribault Club hosts the Fort George Island visitor center and exhibits about the Mocama and later inhabitants. It was built in 1928 as part of a resort.

SITE OF THE MISSION OF
SAN JUAN DEL PUERTO
(Continued From Reverse Side) -
conflict between Florida's Spanish inhabitants
and English and French invaders. In 1696,
Jonathan Dickinson, a Philadelphia Quaker who
had been shipwrecked off the coast of Florida,
passed this way and recorded a visit to "the
town of St. Wan's, a large town and many people."
In 1702, Governor James Moore of the British
Colony of South Carolina attempted to take
St. Augustine from the Spanish. His effort
failed, but in the process of the raid into
Spanish territory, Moore destroyed the Spanish
missions from St. Augustine northward, including
the Mission of San Juan del Puerto.

SPONSORED BY JACKSONVILLE HISTORICAL SOCIETY
IN COOPERATION WITH DEPARTMENT OF STATE

Top: *The historic Ribault Club.*
Inset: *Mission San Juan del Puerto historical marker.*

sometime after 1568, and Alicamani replaced his capital as the chiefdom's leading town. In 1587, the Mocama submitted to the Spanish. Franciscan friars established three missions among them, including San Juan del Puerto (St. John of the Harbor) at Alicamani. The town came to be known by this name, and in turn, the river became *San Juan*, or St. Johns in English.

San Juan del Puerto was one of the largest and longest surviving missions in Spanish Florida, as well as a cultural center for Christianized Mocama. Missionary Francisco Pareja developed a Timucua writing system and published several works, including a Spanish-Timucua catechism that was the first book published in a native language in the present-day US. San Juan del Puerto was abandoned in 1702 following devastating raids by the British, and the last documented Timucua speakers joined the Spanish when they pulled out of Florida in 1763. Though the Timucua are gone, the works in their language offer a glimpse of their lost culture.

BLACKROCK BEACH (BONEYARD BEACH)

What causes the black rocks and tree skeletons to congregate on Big Talbot Island?

A unique natural treasure lies on Big Talbot Island in the Timucuan Ecological and Historic Preserve. Blackrock Beach is picturesque not only for the unusual rocky formations that give it its name but also for the hundreds of bleached skeletons of fallen trees that litter its shore.

The black rock formations, looking like something from a volcanic beach or alien planet, occur all along the shore of Big Talbot facing the Nassau Sound, below the high bluff. Scientifically speaking, they're a type of soil known as *spodosol*, comprising organic matter, iron, and aluminum. Spodosols are common in Florida, but the Big Talbot examples are a rare variety featuring a thick hardpan layer—the black rock. Known as Cornelia, it's one of the rarest types of soil in the world.

The formations on Blackrock Beach developed eons ago in a coastal environment dominated then, as now, by oaks and scrub. As a barrier island, Big Talbot is in a state of slow but constant flux, being shaped and reshaped by erosion and accretion. These forces both expose the spodosol and erode the bluff above the beach, which is topped by a thick live oak hammock. In times past, the oak forest was likely further

Spodosol formations like those at Blackrock Beach also occur on Fort George island around the Mount Cornelia area, but not on any of the area's other barrier islands.

Top: *The "black rock," or hardpan spodosol formations.* Bottom: *A driftwood skeleton on Blackrock Beach.*

BLACKROCK BEACH (BONEYARD BEACH)

WHAT: A beach strewn with unusual rocky formations and driftwood skeletons

WHERE: A trailhead off A1A on Big Talbot Island provides access to the Blackrock Trail leading to the beach.

COST: Free

PRO TIP: Due to erosion, it can be difficult to climb up and down the bluff to reach the beach, so be prepared to bushwhack if need be.

inland, protected from the wind and water. But as the bluff erodes, oaks collapse onto the beach, where they are stripped and bleached white by salt and sun. In death, these driftwood skeletons protect other trees by helping to break up the wind and slowing further erosion. The surreal ambiance they provide also gives the area its alternative name, Boneyard Beach, and makes it one of the best places in Northeast Florida to take pictures. Today, Blackrock Beach serves as a trailhead for the Timucuan Trail, part of the East Coast Greenway.

**LIFT EV'RY VOICE AND SING PARK:
BIRTHPLACE OF AN ANTHEM** (page 24)

JIFFY FEET DON'T FAIL ME NOW (page 62)

TREATY OAK—JACKSONVILLE'S
OLDEST RESIDENT (page 72)

MARINELAND (page 190)

SEXY REXY, KING OF BEACH BOULEVARD (page 160)

SALLY DARK RIDES (page 30)

CHAMBLIN'S, A BOOKLOVER'S LABYRINTH (page 8)

MAYPORT VILLAGE (page 174)

**OLD TOWN: THE ORIGINAL LOCATION
OF FERNANDINA** (page 108)

DUVAL BASS: THE MIAMI BASS SOUND IN JACKSONVILLE (page 10)

The mural names include:

Willie Smith
George Carey
Phillip Faucett
Walter "Skip" Menotte
Kenneth "Kenjo" Pezza
David Wayne Scarboro
John Sistrunk
Michael Baker
Greg Magully
Bobby Reed
Jack Riggin
Steve Young

William Herndon
Tony O'Connor
Daniel Hawarah
Steven Childress
John B. Corcoran II

Douglas Hanson
Ben Summerville
Todd Ashley Scott
Lee Richard Stuart
Malcolm Melton, Jr.
Michael (Bear) Nori
John Beckman
James Larisay

Bob Nichols
James Owens
Dale Griffis
Scott Penny
Jeremy Lucas

WILLOWBRANCH PARK:
JACKSONVILLE'S LGBTQ HOLY GROUND (page 64)

MUSSALLEM GALLERIES: RUGS, FINE ART, AND ANTIQUITIES (page 162)

BULLS BAY PRESERVE AND WATERFALL (page 124)

AMERICAN BEACH: FLORIDA'S FIRST BLACK-OWNED BEACH RESORT

Where did African American Jaxsons access the beach in the days of segregation?

Northeast Florida's beaches have been an international draw since the 19th century, but during the Jim Crow era, African Americans were largely shut out of them. Black beachgoers carved out spaces to enjoy the ocean in more remote areas, including Jacksonville's Manhattan Beach and St. Augustine's Butler Beach. In 1935, the region got something it had never seen before: a Black-owned oceanfront resort community.

American Beach was developed by a group of African American businessmen from Jacksonville, including Abraham Lincoln Lewis, founder of the Afro-American Life Insurance company and Florida's first Black millionaire. Located on Amelia Island about 8 miles south of Fernandina Beach, it featured affordable vacation homes and a cluster of Black-owned restaurants, nightclubs, hotels, and shops. During its glory days from the 1930s into the 1960s, American Beach was the preeminent vacation destination for African Americans in northern Florida. Zora Neale Hurston (see page 36), Hank Aaron (page 50),

AMERICAN BEACH

WHAT: Historic African American beach

WHERE: On Amelia Island roughly between Ocean Boulevard and Gregg, Lewis, Leonard, Main, and James streets

COST: Free

PRO TIP: American Beach's Burney Park offers a quieter beachgoing experience than many of Nassau County's popular beaches.

Top: *Vacation houses at American Beach.* Inset: *Historical marker at NaNa Dune.*

Ray Charles, and Duke Ellington were among those who vacationed at American Beach.

American Beach declined after 1964, when Hurricane Dora destroyed several structures and the Civil Rights Act opened other beaches to African Americans. Over time, development encroached upon the community, and some homes fell into disrepair, but American Beach endured. In 1977, Abraham Lincoln Lewis's granddaughter, opera singer MaVynee Betsch, moved in permanently. Beloved locally as the "Beach Lady," she gave her money to charity and lived primarily on a chaise lounge on the shore. Until her death in 2005, she worked fervently to preserve American Beach's legacy and remaining sites, including the NaNa Dune, the tallest sand dune in Florida. Thanks largely to the Beach Lady's efforts, American Beach was named a historic district, with NaNa one of its landmarks. Today, there's a public beach access, and a small museum dedicated to the area's history opened in 2014.

At 60 feet tall, NaNa Dune is Florida's tallest remaining sand dune and a major part of Amelia Island's protective dune system.

107

OLD TOWN: THE ORIGINAL LOCATION OF FERNANDINA

Why did a town move a mile away?

Most cities, even historic ones, change over time. Fernandina Beach is one of the few that actually changed places. Though far less known than the current city core around Centre Street, Old Town Fernandina still exists, and it's well worth a visit.

Located a mile north of the modern city center, Old Town predates the formal founding of Fernandina Beach. During Florida's British period, the site was the headquarters of the Egmont Plantation, which covered most of Amelia Island. Lord Egmont planned a "New Settlement" there, but little growth occurred after his death in 1770. In 1811, after Spain retook control of Florida, the Spanish chose this area as the location for the new town of Fernandina. The last town planned under Spain's Law of the Indies, it included a small lunette fortification called Fort San Carlos, a central plaza, and gridded streets. Some streets retain their original names, or anglicized versions. Ladies Street, originally Paseo de las Damas, is so called as it was home to women who followed the garrison as prostitutes and laborers.

Railroads sealed Old Town's fate. Former senator and Confederate secessionist David Levy Yulee formed the Florida

Fernandina Plaza Historic State Park is administered as part of the much wider Fort Clinch State Park. For more info, visit floridastateparks.org.

Left: *The Captain's House, also known as the Pippi Longstocking House.* Inset: *Fernandina Plaza, the center of Old Town.*

railroad in 1861, connecting Fernandina to Cedar Key. Yulee determined that the salt marsh around Old Town prevented the railway from extending there, so he established his Fernandina station a mile to the south. After the Civil War, "New Town" grew up around the station and quickly eclipsed the original city center.

Fort San Carlos was gradually destroyed by erosion, but the plaza remains and is now a state park. Old Town carried on as a residential neighborhood. One of Fernandina's most beautiful buildings, the Captain's House, stands east of the plaza. Built in the 1870s as the residence of Fernandina's harbor pilot, it is sometimes called the Pippi Longstocking House after a 1988 movie filmed there.

OLD TOWN FERNANDINA

WHAT: Original site of the town of Fernandina

WHERE: Around the plaza at 715 San Fernando St., Fernandina Beach

COST: Free

PRO TIP: For a historic fort that's still around, visit the nearby Fort Clinch.

BIRTHPLACE OF MODERN SHRIMPING

How did the First Coast revolutionize the shrimping industry?

Shrimp have always been abundant in the waters of the First Coast, with the St. Johns River being a fertile breeding ground. The Mocama Timucua people caught shrimp with cast nets, and during the 19th century, locals used seine nets strung between two rowboats. In the early 20th century, fishermen in Fernandina introduced several innovations that changed the international shrimping industry forever.

Around 1903, Sollecito Salvador was the first to shrimp with a motorboat, allowing him to go further and haul in bigger catches. Other local shrimpers followed suit, pushing further from shore. In 1912, fisherman Billy Corkum made an even bigger innovation. He adapted a New England otter trawl—a basketlike net with boards holding the mouth open as it's dragged behind a boat—for use in Fernandina waters. Initially intending to catch fish, he was stunned at the trawl's effectiveness for shrimp. Other locals made additional modifications to the otter trawl, and within a few years, trawls replaced seine nets as the worldwide industry standard.

Shrimping became Fernandina's main industry, with more than a hundred shrimp boats working from the Front Street docks. As innovations from Fernandina spread, shrimping became the most

Locals commonly talk about "Mayport shrimp." Although the boats mostly port around Mayport, the shrimp are caught across the Southeastern coast.

The Dying Breed, *a shrimp boat based in Mayport*

SHRIMPING MUSEUM

WHAT: Museum celebrating Fernandina's shrimping history

WHERE: 235 S Front St., Fernandina Beach

COST: Free (donations are welcome)

PRO TIP: For good prices on great local shrimp, check out Atlantic Seafood in Fernandina and Safe Harbor in Mayport.

important fishery throughout the First Coast's fishing communities, including in St. Augustine and Mayport (see page 174). Mayport especially became a center with seafood companies distributing local catch across the region.

Unfortunately, since the 1990s local shrimping has declined due to loss of dock space and the influx of imported factory-farmed shrimp. Nonetheless, a number of shrimpers still persevere in local waters, catering to connoisseurs seeking out good Mayport shrimp. While only a handful of shrimpers ply the waters from Fernandina today, in 2014, the town established the Shrimping Museum to tell the story of the First Coast's role in establishing the modern shrimping industry.

THE PALACE SALOON: FLORIDA'S OLDEST BAR

How did this Fernandina Beach watering hole survive Prohibition?

Dating to 1903, Fernandina Beach's Palace Saloon is the oldest bar anywhere in Florida. Though a few other bars across the state make the same claim, the Palace Saloon is the oldest that's kept its original location and name. But how did this iconic saloon survive for over a century—including through Prohibition?

The main reason is that its owners managed to stand out from the crowd in every generation. When the Palace Saloon opened, there were 24 other bars in Fernandina, most catering to sailors. German-born barman Louis G. Hirth decided to offer something folks couldn't get anywhere else in town: an upscale saloon for the town's elite, ship officers, and wealthy visitors, complete with a hand-carved English oak bar and classic tin ceiling.

THE PALACE SALOON

WHAT: Florida's oldest bar

WHERE: 117 Centre St., Fernandina Beach

COST: The price of a drink

PRO TIP: The Palace Saloon hosts live music during the weekends.

When Prohibition took effect in 1919, the Palace Saloon was reportedly the last bar in Florida to close. To survive, Hirth shifted his offerings to ice cream and low-alcohol wines and "near beers." When Prohibition was repealed in 1933, Hirth brought back liquor, though the bar was much less successful this time. Hirth died in 1938, and his estate ran the bar until 1956, seeing continually diminishing sales. In 1957, Dee Land and Ervin Williams bought the struggling bar and restored it as an old-time saloon with many of its original furnishings. By looking

The Palace Saloon

to the past, Land and Williams again made the Palace something unique and special in town.

This same spirit of adaptability has allowed the Palace to weather further challenges through the years, including a fire in 1999 and the COVID-19 pandemic. By combining both a dedication to history and the flexibility to adapt to changing times, the Palace Saloon is perhaps the perfect model for historic preservation.

Among the colorful characters inhabiting the Palace Saloon is bartender Johnny Miller, who in addition to slinging drinks served as a Fernandina Beach City Commissioner from 2013 to 2020.

WICCADEMOUS, THE WITCH OF FERNANDINA

Does a witch haunt the woods near Fernandina Beach High School?

For decades, teenagers from all over Northeast Florida have trekked to a strip of woods across from Fernandina Beach High School in search of a marvel: the secret grave of a supposed 17th-century witch known by the unlikely name of Wiccademous. Along with Annie Lytle School (page 58) and Ghost Light Road (page 178), it has been one of the region's primary locales for teenagers in search of a scare.

Fernandina Beach High School moved to Citrona Drive in 1957, with the current building dating to 1991. The woods across the street were owned by the school but left undeveloped for decades. The space earned a reputation for strange happenings, and by the 1970s and 1980s, teenagers were making regular trips.

Early legends apparently didn't include a witch. The place was known as "Shaky Ground," as it was said that the earth would quake beneath a visitor's feet. Some locals attributed this to an old underground mill drainpipe, while others preferred a supernatural explanation. Eventually, a story emerged that the rumbling ground was caused by "Wiccademous," the angry spirit of a girl executed for witchcraft in the 17th century and buried beneath an oak tree. This

---

THE WICCADEMOUS "GRAVE": EGANS CREEK GREENWAY'S HICKORY STREET ENTRANCE

WHAT: A wooded area said to be the grave of Wiccademous, a vengeful 17th-century witch

WHERE: The trailhead is east of the intersection of Hickory Street and Citrona Drive

COST: Free

PRO TIP: The Hickory Street trailhead is a great place to jump onto the Egans Creek Greenway.

One of the few remaining strands of the woods said to be haunted by Wiccademous

farrago of witchy tropes exploded in popularity after it first appeared online in 2002, becoming cemented in local folklore and drawing further attention to the woods.

In 2019, the land was controversially sold to a developer and platted out for a new subdivision. The legend has not died, however, and teenagers still trek to what remains of the woods in hopes of encountering Wiccademous; one particular strand off the trail leading to the Egans Creek Greenway (see page 116) is popular. This is a case where the legend created to explain a scary place has survived in local imagination even after the place itself is gone.

Two other witches haunt Fernandina folklore. Filipa the Witch was a Gullah Geechee root doctor in 19th-century Old Town (page 108), and eccentric 20th-century Crane Island resident Sarah Alice Broadbent was also dubbed a witch.

EGANS CREEK GREENWAY: A NATURAL REFUGE IN THE HEART OF FERNANDINA BEACH

Where can you see native wildlife in the middle of a town?

Amid the suburban sprawl of Fernandina Beach is the Egans Creek Greenway. This linear park encompasses several miles of natural space around the creek and 5.6 miles of trails through two different environments: freshwater forest to the south and a wide tidal salt marsh to the north.

Previously known as Anderson's Creek and Clark's Creek, Egans Creek starts just north of present-day Sadler Road and flows north for three miles before turning west into the Amelia River. Native Americans periodically occupied the area around the creek's mouth as early as 2000 BC, and in the 1770s, this area was the headquarters of the vast Egmont slave plantation, which included most of Amelia Island. The creek's present name derives from Stephen Egan, an Irish administrator who ran the Egmont plantation after the Earl of Egmont's death in 1770. In 1811, the Spanish platted the town of Fernandina, specifically the area known as Old Town (see page 108), on the site.

By the mid-20th century, suburban sprawl had consumed Egans Creek. In an effort to control flooding and mosquitos, the

Named for a local advocate and bird-watcher, the Eleanor Latimer Colborn Bridge allows access to the greenway from Hickory Street.

An alligator in Egans Creek

EGANS CREEK GREENWAY

WHAT: A linear park

WHERE: There are several access points: the Atlantic Recreation Center at 2500 Atlantic Ave., at Hickory and Beech Streets off Citrona Drive, the Jasmine Street access between Citrona Drive and Fletcher Avenue, and behind the Residence Inn at 2301 Sadler Rd. The Jasmine Street entrance allows access to both the north and south sections of the greenway.

COST: Free

PRO TIP: Bring a camera or binoculars, as this is an excellent place to see birds.

government diked the creek and channeled it into retention ditches, destroying its salt marsh environment in the process. In 1996, the City of Fernandina Beach launched an ambitious project to acquire acres of land in order to restore the creek and create a public greenway. Egans Creek Greenway opened in 2000, and the project successfully reconnected the creek to the Amelia River's tidal flow in 2003, bringing back the salt marsh ecology for the first time in half a century.

Today, the Egans Creek Greenway is one of Fernandina's most popular parks, and it's an excellent place to see native Northeast Florida wildlife in the heart of a growing community.

WHITE OAK CONSERVATION

How did rural Nassau County become a sanctuary for endangered animals and the global elite alike?

On the banks of the St. Marys River, there's a place where political leaders, actors, musicians, and dancers congregate while zoologists tend to endangered creatures. Comprising 16,000 acres of woods, wetlands, and amenities, White Oak Conservation is a world unto itself.

The property's history begins with the White Oak slave plantation, established in 1768. Its main crop was rice, and remains of its paddies can still be seen. Zephaniah Kingsley of the Kingsley Plantation (see page 80) owned White Oak Plantation from 1833 to 1842; it was largely abandoned after the Civil War. In 1938, the Gilman Paper Company, owned by Charles Gilman, acquired the former plantation along with thousands of acres of timberland in Georgia and Florida. In 1982, Gilman's son Howard became the sole owner of the St. Marys-based company. An eccentric millionaire with a strong interest in philanthropy, Howard Gilman spent $154 million transforming White Oak into his personal Xanadu. He built a golf course, a conference center, and a state-of-the-art dance studio for Mikhail Baryshnikov. Guests included Bill and Hillary Clinton, Colin Powell, Al Gore, Isabella Rossellini, and Madonna.

Most notably, Gilman dedicated 700 acres to a sanctuary for endangered and threatened animals. The conservation center introduced breeding programs and training for animal specialists to

The conference center has elaborate exhibits of art as well as fossils of dinosaurs and other extinct creatures.

Top: *A rhino at White Oak Conservation.* Inset: *Fossil exhibit at the White Oak Conservation conference center.* Photos by Gena Delaney

help save populations in distress. Gilman died in 2003, and in 2013, White Oak was sold to conservation-minded billionaires Mark and Kimbra Walter, who manage wildlife refuges across the world. Today, White Oak Conservation hosts species that include reticulated giraffes, okapis, rhinoceroses, cheetahs, and Florida panthers. In 2021, White Oak started building a 2,500-acre free-range habitat for retired circus elephants. The first habitat of its kind in the United States, it is expected to house 35 endangered Asian elephants, the largest herd in the Americas.

WHITE OAK CONSERVATION

WHAT: Animal sanctuary

WHERE: 581705 White Oak Rd., Yulee

COST: Tours are $100 for adults, $50 for kids.

PRO TIP: The best time for a tour is at dusk, when the animals are most active.

CUMBERLAND ISLAND

Where can you see wild horses and gothic ruins?

Only 30 miles northeast of Downtown Jacksonville (as the crow flies, anyway) lies a truly magical island full of sights that can't be found anywhere else. Designated a National Seashore, Cumberland Island features miles of pristine beaches, trails through dense maritime forests, gothic ruins, and even its own band of feral horses. No bridge connects it to the mainland; it can only be reached by boat. Most visits are by ferry, which runs to the island from the docks at St. Marys, Georgia, twice a day.

Cumberland's human history starts at least 4,000 years ago with the arrival of the Mocama Timucua (see page 84). At the time of European contact, Cumberland Island was the capital of the Tacatacuru chiefdom, which was eventually incorporated into the Spanish mission system. When the British colonized Georgia in 1733, the island became a strategic location at the border with Spanish Florida. It was later used as a slave plantation, and after the

CUMBERLAND ISLAND NATIONAL SEASHORE

WHAT: Protected barrier island

WHERE: Camden County, Georgia; access by ferry at the Visitor Center: 113 St. Marys St. W, St. Marys, GA

COST: $10, plus $30 dollars for a ferry ticket

PRO TIP: The ferry only runs twice a day, so make sure you don't miss it.

Cumberland Island is a great place to camp. There's also a lone hotel on the island, the historic Greyfield Inn, originally built by the Carnegies.

Top: *The Dungeness ruins.* Inset: *Feral horse at Cumberland Island.*

Civil War, it was home to Gullah Geechee communities (see also page 148); otherwise, it saw little development.

In the 1880s, industrialist Thomas Carnegie purchased land on Cumberland for a family winter home. The family built several residences, starting with the main mansion, Dungeness. This burned down in 1959, and its ruins now stand as a sublime backdrop to an already picturesque landscape. With the island at risk of being developed, the Carnegies sold most of the land to the National Parks Service to form the Cumberland Island National Seashore in 1972.

Perhaps the most noted feature of Cumberland Island is the band of horses, which numbers about 150. Their roots may trace back to the 18th century if not to the Spanish period. They can be seen throughout the island wandering the trails and ruins.

OKEFENOKEE SWAMP: LAND OF THE TREMBLING EARTH

Where can you see the largest wildlife refuge on the East Coast?

It's fairly well known that Jacksonville has more park and preserve land than any other city, with 80,000 acres. Less well known is the fact that just outside the city are some of the greatest natural spaces in the country. Straddling the Florida–Georgia border less than an hour west of the city is the Okefenokee Swamp, the largest national wildlife refuge in the Eastern United States.

The Okefenokee is one of the largest intact freshwater systems in the world, as its impenetrable nature made it impractical for engineers to drain. It's a refuge for hundreds of native bird, animal, and plant species, including endangered longleaf pines, gopher tortoises, indigo snakes, and wood storks (see page 56). Other common animals include alligators, bobcats, turtles, river otters, and more than 200 bird species.

The Okefenokee has a long human history and a prominent place in the region's culture and folklore. In the 17th century, it was home to the Oconi Timucua. Later, it became a haven for Muscogee and Seminole peoples, who gave it its current name; Okefenokee roughly means "Land of the Trembling Earth" in

OKEFENOKEE NATIONAL WILDLIFE REFUGE

WHAT: Protected swamp

WHERE: There are three main entrances. The closest to Jacksonville is Suwannee Canal Recreation Area off Highway 121/23 near Folkston, GA.

COST: $5 per vehicle

PRO TIP: The other Okefenokee entrances are also worth checking out, though they're a bit farther away.

Okefenokee Swamp

Muscogee, in reference to the swamp's many unstable peat masses that quiver when stepped upon. For centuries, the Okefenokee's dense forests and labyrinthine waters made it a frequent hiding place for Native Americans, enslaved African Americans, and others evading the authorities. Both Native Americans and European Americans told stories of the swamp being inhabited by a mystical, immortal race of people.

From the 1860s into the 1920s, the Okefenokee saw substantial changes as railroads encircled and penetrated the deep swamp, allowing for logging and turpentine operations to encroach on it. Subsequently, efforts were made to preserve the Okefenokee as a national wildlife refuge. There are three main entry points, each with its own amenities and sights.

Find out more about the Okefenokee National Wildlife Refuge at fws.gov/refuge/okefenokee.

BULLS BAY PRESERVE AND WATERFALL

What does a Florida waterfall look like?

One of Jacksonville's best kept secrets, Bulls Bay Preserve on the Westside quietly opened to the public in 2019. Containing Bulls Bay Swamp, it is the source of two significant St. Johns River tributaries, Sixmile Creek and the Cedar River.

In the 19th century, it was known as the Cracker Swamp after its main inhabitants, the rustic white Floridians called "crackers." Before the Civil War, the swamp was part of the vast Paradise Plantation, owned by Isaiah D. Hart. Hart started out as a slave raider who kidnapped and sold off free and enslaved African Americans; he then used these earnings to become a major real estate baron. He carved the original city of Jacksonville out of part of his property in 1822.

After the Civil War, Hart's son Ossian disposed of Paradise, and it was subsequently used for timber, cattle farming, and sand mining. In the late 20th century, it was a popular teenage hangout dubbed "The Pits." Development steadily threatened Bulls Bay before the state put it under the protection of the St. Johns River Water Management District (SJRWMD) in the 1970s. To save it, in 1999 the city acquired more than 1,200 acres of the swamp from its owners as part of the Preservation Project, which ultimately assembled 51,000 acres of protected natural land across the city. However, SJRWMD restrictions precluded its development as a park for more than 20 years.

Nobody knows where Bulls Bay's name comes from. "Bay" may refer not to water but to the bay tree, or to a baygall, a marshy wetland rife with bay trees.

The Bulls Bay waterfall

BULLS BAY PRESERVE

WHAT: A 1,200-acre wetland preserve containing one of Florida's few natural waterfalls

WHERE: 8017 Old Plank Rd.

COST: Free

PRO TIP: Bulls Bay Preserve is the eastern terminus of the Jacksonville-Baldwin Rail Trail. Hike or bike over to Camp Milton or all the way to Baldwin.

In 2019, the city quietly cut trails in a small portion of the preserve. One path leads to a site you can't find in most of Florida: a small natural waterfall. This nameless waterfall drops into a small pool and flows on into the Cedar River and onward to the St. Johns. Located only 10 minutes from Downtown Jacksonville, it's one of the most accessible waterfalls in Florida.

CAMP MILTON

What role did a military camp west of Jacksonville play in the city's fate during the Civil War?

While Florida was a sparsely populated backwater during the Civil War, it saw its share of action, especially in the First Coast. The Union held Fernandina and St. Augustine from March 1862 through the end of the war and occupied Jacksonville four times, including permanently after February 1864. Jacksonville was a hotbed of Unionist sentiment, with many White citizens and virtually all Black citizens supporting the United States. The fourth Union force included several Black regiments, some of whose members came from the region.

Union general Truman Seymour launched an advance into Confederate territory, leading to the Battle of Olustee, Florida's only major Civil War battle, on February 20, 1864. The Confederate victory drove the Union back to Jacksonville. To prevent another Union advance, the Confederates established Camp Milton 12 miles west of Jacksonville as their eastern Florida headquarters. Named for Florida's Confederate governor John Milton, it featured a three-mile-long fortification of earth and wood.

With 8,000 men, Camp Milton was the largest Confederate fort in Florida. Its men sometimes entertained themselves with "battles" in which they threw flaming pine cones at each other. By June 1864, the Confederacy had reassigned most of the

---

CAMP MILTON HISTORIC PRESERVE

WHAT: A park preserving the remains of the Confederate Camp Milton and other attractions

WHERE: 1225 Halsema Rd. N

COST: Free

PRO TIP: Also check out the grove of trees seeded from historic locations, the preserved farmhouse and the 19th-century Florida cracker cabin.

Camp Milton Historic Preserve today

troops. On July 1, the Union captured Camp Milton without a fight and burned down the wooden palisades. Afterward, it saw only intermittent use, and after the war, it was largely forgotten for more than 100 years.

Years of development took out all but 725 feet of the Confederate earthwork, which was identified as Camp Milton in 1973. In 1999, the City of Jacksonville's Preservation Project acquired the site and surrounding acres, keeping them from becoming a sludge field. Camp Milton Historic Preserve opened in 2006, featuring a trail to the earthworks, informational signs, and interpretive structures.

Camp Milton Historic Preserve is on the Jacksonville-Baldwin Rail Trail. From here, visitors can head west to Baldwin or east toward Bulls Bay Preserve (page 124).

JACKSONVILLE'S SOUTHERN ROCK GRAVES

How many Southern rock legends are buried in Jacksonville?

In the 1960s and 1970s, Jacksonville was the birthplace of many prominent Southern rock bands, including the Allman Brothers (see page 68), Lynyrd Skynyrd, and others. Naturally, then, it's also the final resting place of many of the genre's musicians.

Just two cemeteries contain the graves of many of Southern rock's greats. Jacksonville Memory Gardens in Orange Park is home to the original grave of Lynyrd Skynyrd founder Ronnie Van Zant as well as Skynyrd guitarist Steve Gaines and his sister, backup singer Cassie Gaines. All three were among the casualties of the 1977 plane crash that ended the band's first incarnation. Also located in the cemetery is the grave of bassist Larry Junstrom, a founding member of Lynyrd Skynyrd who later joined Van Zant's brother Donnie in the band 38 Special. Van Zant's grave was vandalized in 2000, and his family relocated his remains to Riverside Memorial Park, where other members of the family are buried.

Van Zant's current grave has become a pilgrimage site for fans, who routinely leave flowers and messages. It stands nearby the resting places of three other members of the band. The graves of bassist Leon Wilkeson and pianist Billy Powell are located in the same area as Van Zant's, while guitarist Allen Collins lies in a section across the street.

Ronnie Van Zant grew up at 5419 Woodcrest Road, alongside his brothers: 38 Special guitarist Donnie, and later Lynyrd Skynyrd vocalist Johnnie. A historical plaque marks the house today.

JACKSONVILLE'S SOUTHERN ROCK GRAVES

WHAT: The graves of many Southern rock legends, including Lynyrd Skynyrd frontman Ronnie Van Zant

WHERE: Jacksonville Memory Gardens is located at 111 Blanding Blvd., Orange Park. Riverside Memorial Park is located at 7242 Normandy Blvd.

COST: Free

PRO TIP: Many visitors leave a guitar pick or other item in tribute to the dead rockers.

Top: *Grave of Steve Gaines at Jacksonville Memory Gardens.* Bottom: *Grave of Lynyrd Skynyrd frontman Ronnie Van Zant at Riverside Memorial Park. Photos by Chris Soldt*

Not far from Collins's grave is the burial place of Leonard Skinner, the band's namesake. Skinner was Van Zant and company's gym coach at Lee High School, known for enforcing the school's rules on long hair too strictly for the young musicians' taste. In a tongue-and-cheek homage, they renamed their band after him. Another Southern rocker buried at Riverside Memorial Park is Dave Hlubek, founder and lead guitarist of Jacksonville-based Molly Hatchet.

THE BIRTHPLACE OF THE BLUE ANGELS

How did Naval Air Station (NAS) Jacksonville create a legendary aviation team?

Established in 1940 as the US prepared to enter World War II, Naval Air Station Jacksonville has had an immense impact on its home city. Together with Naval Station Mayport, a major sea base established in 1942 (see page 174), it turned Jacksonville into one of America's biggest Navy cities by the end of the war.

One part of NAS Jacksonville's history that deserves more public recognition is its designation as the birthplace of the Navy's famous demonstration squadron, the Blue Angels.

In 1946, the war was over, and Admiral Chester Nimitz, Chief of Naval Operations, wanted something that would boost morale and inspire citizens' interest in naval aviation during peacetime. To this end, he charged decorated flying ace Roy Voris with building a team of top pilots to show off what the Navy could do. The Navy chose NAS Jacksonville as the demonstration team's inaugural headquarters.

To provide a captivating spectacle, Voris's team practiced innovative aerobatic stunts and devised their show so that the audience would always have something in view. The team held their first private demonstration in June and put on a two-day public show on July 15 and 16. It featured F6F-5 Hellcats painted in

NAS JACKSONVILLE: BIRTHPLACE OF THE BLUE ANGELS

WHAT: Major naval air base

WHERE: 6801 Roosevelt Blvd.

COST: Free

PRO TIP: Base personnel and families can visit Heritage Park anytime, and others can make a reservation. Contact nasjaxpao@navy.mil.

An F/A-18 Blue Angel on display at NAS Jacksonville

the Navy's traditional blue and gold colors and performing death-defying maneuvers. The show was a massive success, and the Navy took the team, soon after named the "Blue Angels," on tour.

The Blue Angels were relocated to NAS Pensacola in 1954, but they maintain a strong presence in Jacksonville with annual airshows at the base and elsewhere that draw hundreds of thousands of spectators. Today, NAS Jacksonville has a retired Blue Angel F/A-18 Hornet on display by the main entrance. Inside the base is Heritage Park, where several other historic aircraft are on display.

NAS Jacksonville is the third-largest US Navy base. Naval Station Mayport and Naval Submarine Base Kings Bay in St. Marys, Georgia, are also major presences in the First Coast.

YUKON: JACKSONVILLE'S GHOST TOWN

What became of the town of Yukon?

Decades ago, Yukon in what's now Westside Jacksonville was a vibrant town. It had its own downtown strip with restaurants, a church, a post office, and a train station, encircled by streets and homes. During the 1960s, it became one of Duval County's most prominent ghost towns, with few reminders that a community had once stood there.

The town grew up on what had been the Mulberry Grove Plantation. Shortly before the Civil War, the plantation's last owner, Arthur Reed, sold a parcel of land to a former slave, Joe Reese. After the war ended slavery, Reed hired many of the freedmen as paid employees, and many of them bought additional plots of land. They formed a community initially known as Black Point Settlement and later as Yukon.

In the early 20th century, Yukon's growth centered around the railroad, which built a passenger stop for the community. A streetcar line also connected Yukon to Jacksonville. In 1917, the Department of War established Camp Joseph E. Johnson near the town, sparking further growth. Parts of the brick-paved roads built in this period can be seen today.

In 1939, the US Navy acquired much of the land east of Roosevelt Boulevard for Naval Air Station Jacksonville. As the station grew into one of the Navy's largest, Yukon's homes

The Yukon Cemetery is located in the woods of Tillie Fowler Park. It contains the graves of enslaved and free Black residents who first established the town.

Top: *Yukon's Downtown business strip is still present today.* Inset: *The old Yukon brick road can still be seen in the woods.*

were increasingly in the flight paths of naval aircraft. In July 1963, the Navy declared Yukon a flight hazard. Most buildings were bought and demolished, and Yukon was no more.

In 1979, the City of Jacksonville leased much of the land from the Navy and established Tillie K. Fowler Regional Park, which features trails, a nature center, and an observation tower. Several buildings on the old downtown strip remain, the only part of Yukon not demolished. Other traces of the former town include a cemetery hidden away in the park.

YUKON

WHAT: A ghost town

WHERE: A few buildings remain on 120th Street west of Roosevelt Boulevard. Other remains can be explored at Tillie K. Fowler Regional Park, 7000 Roosevelt Blvd.

COST: Free

PRO TIP: It doesn't get much better than Trent's Seafood, located in one of Yukon's remaining structures.

WRECK OF
THE *MAPLE LEAF*

What secrets lie at the bottom of the St. Johns River?

By March 1864, at the height of the Civil War, Union forces dominated coastal Florida. In the First Coast, they had controlled Fernandina and St. Augustine since 1862 and had settled into their fourth, permanent occupation of Jacksonville. The Confederates controlled interior Florida, and after the Confederate victory at the Battle of Olustee, the Union ceased substantial missions by land. The St. Johns River became the last battlefront.

US Navy gunboats enabled the Union to dominate the river far south of Jacksonville. Realizing Union naval superiority, the Confederates shifted tactics. On March 30, a Confederate detachment under Captain E. Pliny Bryan placed 12 torpedoes (floating mines) across the river at Mandarin Point. On April 1, the torpedoes claimed their first Northeast Florida casualty: the *Maple Leaf*, a side-wheel steamship employed by the US Army as a transport for troops and cargo. Sailing north to Jacksonville from Palatka before dawn under the guidance of Romeo Murray, a skilled freedman river pilot, the ship expected a quiet trip. But at 3:59 a.m., the ship struck a torpedo. Four died in the blast, and within minutes, the ship had sunk along with hundreds of pounds of cargo.

WRECK OF THE *MAPLE LEAF*

WHAT: Civil War shipwreck in the St. Johns River

WHERE: The wreck is inaccessible, but artifacts can be seen at the Mandarin Museum and the Museum of Science and History.

COST: Price of museum admission

PRO TIP: There are historical markers for the *Maple Leaf* at Orange Park's Kingsley Avenue River Overlook and Downtown Jacksonville's Southbank Riverwalk.

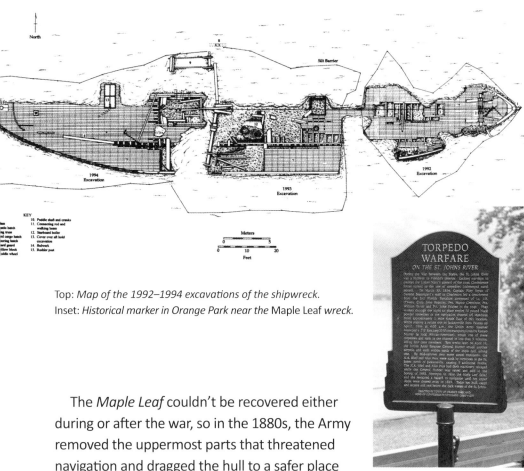

North

Silt Barrier

1994
Excavation

1993
Excavation

1992
Excavation

KEY

Meters
0   5
0   10   20
Feet

Top: *Map of the 1992–1994 excavations of the shipwreck.*
Inset: *Historical marker in Orange Park near the* Maple Leaf *wreck.*

TORPEDO
WARFARE
ON THE ST. JOHNS RIVER

The *Maple Leaf* couldn't be recovered either during or after the war, so in the 1880s, the Army removed the uppermost parts that threatened navigation and dragged the hull to a safer place in the river. There it sat hidden beneath 7 feet of muck and 20 feet of water for nearly a century, its location forgotten. In 1984, a team of divers with St. Johns Archaeological Expeditions rediscovered the shipwreck. The team recovered more than 3,000 artifacts preserved by the muck, making the wreck one of the Civil War's most valuable archaeological sites anywhere.

Three other ships were subsequently lost to Confederate torpedoes on the St. Johns before the Union figured out how to thwart them. Unlike the *Maple Leaf*, they were all raised.

YERKES LABORATORIES OF PRIMATE BIOLOGY— BEHOLD THE HUMANZEE

Was a half-human, half-chimp hybrid born in an Orange Park laboratory?

Unseen and unknown by most in the region, from 1930 to 1965, the town of Orange Park was home to one of the largest chimpanzee research operations in the world. The lab was founded by Yale primatologist Robert M. Yerkes, who wanted a warm, inexpensive location to rear and study captive chimps. Over the years, many renowned scientists worked there on subjects such as chimpanzee anatomy, behavior, and cognition. The facility comprised 200 acres, although only 10 were developed into buildings to house and study the apes.

Staff sometimes brought chimps around town, but otherwise didn't interact much with the community. To locals, the "Monkey Farm" was a mysterious place, the subject of rumors and hushed conversations. In 1965, Yale transferred the Yerkes Labs to Emory University, who relocated it to Atlanta. Developer Marvin Wilhite purchased the Orange Park property, building a subdivision on the undeveloped acreage. Unusually in demolition-happy Northeast Florida, he kept the old lab buildings for an office park. Businesses now operate where experiments once occurred; the caretaker's house is now the Granary, a health food shop.

Yerkes Labs wasn't the only place said to have experimented with chimp-human hybrids. Soviet scientist Ilya Ivanovich Ivanov openly tried to create a humanzee in the 1920s.

Artist Sam Scavino's take on the humanzee

YERKES
LABORATORIES
OF PRIMATE BIOLOGY

This forgotten history is interesting enough, but the Yerkes lab has entered the realm of legend due to the claim that an extremely unorthodox experiment occurred there. According to University of Albany professor Dr. Gordon Gallup, a colleague who worked at the Yerkes lab in the early days told him stories of what went on there. The colleague told Gallup that the scientists successfully impregnated a female chimpanzee with human sperm, creating a hybrid "humanzee," but the scientists euthanized him after birth because of the ethical implications of his existence.

This story became embedded in local lore shortly after Gallup related it in a 2003 documentary about humanzees. There's no other evidence such an experiment took place, but no matter. It's firmly part of the legacy of what's now the most intriguing office park in Florida.

GREEN COVE SPRING PARK

How did an ancient mineral spring create a town?

The large, warm sulfur spring that gives Green Cove Springs its name has attracted human interest for thousands of years. Archaeology shows that Native Americans fished and hunted in the area as early as 3000 BC. In the mid-19th century, the spring gained a reputation for health and wellness, eventually causing a town to "spring" up as well.

Only about 20 settlers lived in the area in 1860. This changed rapidly after the Civil War when word got out about White Sulfur Spring, as it was then called. Promoters extolled its healing effects; some even claimed it was the true Fountain of Youth (see page 184). In short order, hotels and steamship docks cropped up, catering to tourists seeking out the spring's purported health benefits. By 1869, the population had boomed so much that a town was platted out, with the area surrounding the spring designated as public park space. To accommodate the huge influx of visitors, the hotels diverted the spring run into a larger swimming pool away from the springhead.

GREEN COVE SPRING PARK

WHAT: A public pool around a mineral spring

WHERE: 106 St. Johns Ave., Green Cove Springs

COST: $5 for a day pass

PRO TIP: Check out the waterfall on the east end of the pool where the water flows into the St. Johns River.

The Green Cove Springs Historic District includes 78 historic buildings in addition to Spring Pool, the only structure in the district that's not a building.

Top: *Green Cove Spring flows into the Spring Park pool.* Inset: *Water flows out from the pool down a waterfall and then out to the St. Johns River.*

In the 1890s, Green Cove Springs' tourist economy collapsed as railroad expansion brought visitors further south, and in the 1930s, the decline was compounded by the Great Depression. Then, in 1938, the Works Progress Administration (WPA), a federal infrastructure project of the New Deal, endeavored to rebuild the spring and pool. The project built a new City Hall as well as new infrastructure for the Spring Pool. WPA workers built a basin around the spring and established the current setup wherein the spring run flows into a 25- by 70-foot public pool and then out to the St. Johns River.

BARDIN BOOGER

Does an apelike creature stalk the woods around Bardin, Florida?

Bardin, a small Putnam County logging community with a population of 424, isn't the kind of place that usually attracts a lot of nationwide interest. Since 1981, however, one resident has consistently drawn in news crews, writers, and monster hunters: the legendary Bardin Booger.

Sightings of strange things in the Bardin woods go back many decades. Descriptions of the Booger have varied, but generally they fit the mold of the Skunk Ape, Florida's version of Bigfoot. Stories swapped at Bud's Grocery, the superette at the center of town, depict a huge, hairy wildman who menaces those who breach his forest domain.

By 1981, the legend had spread enough to draw the attention of *Palatka Daily News* publisher Jody Delzell. When an intern needed a topic for a column one day, Delzell suggested Bardin's beast. It was Delzell who coined the "Bardin Booger" name, "booger" being another term for "boogieman."

The column took off well beyond Putnam County, and within days, national news outlets were flocking to the rural community to cover its famous Booger. Locals embraced the attention and amused themselves by taking news crews on wild goose chases in search of the creature, and Bud's Grocery became the Booger seekers' mecca, even stocking Booger-themed merchandise.

Sightings dried up not long after this spate of coverage, but some locals have kept the legend alive. For years, Delzell

BARDIN

WHAT: A small town with its own cryptid

WHERE: Rural Putnam County

COST: Free

PRO TIP: You just might see Lena Crain's version of Boog at a parade or event in the Palatka area.

Lena Crain in her Bardin Booger costume. Photo courtesy of Lena Crain

wrote columns based on his conversations with the wise old Booger, and local musician Billy Crain wrote a song about him that became popular at local bars. Billy's wife Lena Crain devised a Booger costume so the creature could make public appearances at events and festivals. She has continued appearing as "Ol' Boog" for nearly 40 years, ensuring the next generation remembers the legend that once brought the international media to their quiet town.

Bud's Grocery keeps a "Booger File" of all the press the creature has generated over the years. Ask to take a look.

EXCHANGE CLUB ISLAND (MUD ISLAND)

How do you get to the island under the Mathews Bridge?

Thousands of people drive over one of Jacksonville's most singular parks without ever realizing it. Though it hasn't always been accessible or maintained, the island under the Mathews Bridge is an official city park.

Originally known as Mud Island, this 34-acre tract is not a natural feature of the St. Johns River. It formed around 1940 from sediment raised when the shipping channel was dredged. Though it is officially state property, in 1941, an enterprising old salt, Captain Augustus Swan, decided to moor his houseboat by the shore and stay. Swan lived a quiet squatter's life there until passing away in 1949. Subsequently, fisherman R. H. Jones and his wife "Tugboat Annie" made the island their home until 1955. In 1953, the Mathews Bridge was built directly over the island.

In 1956, a local civic group named the Exchange Club offered to help make Mud Island into a park. The State of Florida transferred it to the City of Jacksonville, and soon a wood-frame building, picnic areas, bathrooms, and small harbors for boats were added. The island was renamed Exchange Club Island after its benefactors, and for a brief while, it was an idyllic space. Unfortunately, the new park was beset by vandals and looters who

Many locals believe the island is swarming with rattlesnakes, although others report not having seen any in years. Either way, the reputation helped keep people away during its wilderness years.

EXCHANGE CLUB ISLAND (MUD ISLAND)

WHAT: A 34-acre manmade island in the St. Johns River maintained as a city park

WHERE: The St. Johns River below the Mathews Bridge. The nearest boat ramp is the Arlington Public Boat Ramp at 5100–5210 Arlington Rd.

COST: Free

PRO TIP: The pavilions are a great place for a picnic, but bring a good pair of shoes, as there are lots of spurs and cactuses about.

damaged the buildings, stole the barbecue grills, and left heaps of beer cans and trash. The city cleaned it up several times before calling it quits in 1972, capping the artesian well and leaving the island to nature.

There were several proposals for new uses of Exchange Club Island, but these went nowhere until 2014, when the city decided to restore it as an actively maintained park for the first time in 40 years. In 2017, the renovated park opened with a floating dock, kayak launch, pavilions, and trails.

NORMAN STUDIOS AND SILENT FILM'S WINTER CAPITAL

What's left of Jacksonville's days as an epicenter of the silent film industry?

Before Hollywood, the film industry had Jacksonville. In the early days of silent film, New York studios needed places to shoot during wintertime, and from 1908 to 1922, Jacksonville served as film's "Winter Capital." The city was home to more than 30 film studios that produced nearly 300 films, including the first Technicolor film.

The film business's influence caused tension among citizens. In 1917, voters elected an anti-film mayor over major film supporter J. E. T. Bowden. At the same time, Hollywood was emerging as a feasible location for year-round filming, and New York studios were pulling up stakes. The Jacksonville movie industry's fate was sealed, and nearly all the city's studios shuttered by 1920.

Jacksonville's silent film story doesn't end there, however. In 1920, Richard Norman bought the former Eagle Film City studio complex, built in 1916 in Arlington. Norman, a 29-year-old White filmmaker, carved out a niche by making films for the neglected Black audience, featuring Black casts. Over the next decade,

Silent film stars who made movies in Jacksonville include Theda Bara, Rudolph Valentino, and Mary Pickford. Oliver Hardy of Laurel and Hardy fame broke into film in Jacksonville as well.

The Norman Studios main building

Norman Studios produced eight feature-length movies and several shorts; their best known (and only surviving) picture was *The Flying Ace*, which tells the story of a heroic African American World War I pilot.

Norman's silent film studio became obsolete with the advent of sound films in the late 1920s. The complex was spared the fate met by all of Jacksonville's other shuttered studios as the Norman family retained ownership; Richard Norman continued distributing films, and his wife Gloria Norman used the complex for a dance studio until 1974. Subsequently, the property was parceled out and sold off, and the buildings fell into serious disrepair. In 1999, the City of Jacksonville acquired and restored four of the buildings, and they now serve as a museum dedicated to Norman Studios and Jacksonville's lost silent film legacy.

NORMAN STUDIOS SILENT FILM MUSEUM

WHAT: Silent film museum in the old Norman property

WHERE: 6337 Arlington Rd.

COST: Varies by event

PRO TIP: Check the calendar for showings of silent films, including *The Flying Ace*.

KONA SKATEPARK, SKATEBOARDING MECCA

Where is the oldest private skatepark in the US?

Many locals know that skateboarding is a popular pastime in Jacksonville. Fewer know that the city is home to a park some consider the Mecca of skateboarding: Kona, the oldest surviving privately owned skatepark in the country.

Skateboarding emerged in Southern California in the early 1950s, with the first purpose-built skateparks appearing in 1965. By about 1970, street skateboarding had taken off in Jacksonville, and skateparks soon followed, among the earliest on the East Coast. Kona opened in 1977 as part of that first wave. Built on a dunefield near Regency Mall in the neighborhood known as Woodland Acres or Sin City, Kona distinguished itself through its size and design. One of the larger skateparks of the time, it featured concrete hills, a steep bowl, pools, a long snake run, and

KONA SKATEPARK

WHAT: The oldest privately owned skatepark in the US

WHERE: 8739 Kona Ave.

COST: $5 registration plus $10 daily admission

PRO TIP: You'll need your own helmet and pads to skate Kona. You can buy them at the shop.

The first recorded elevator drop—where a skater drops straight down off a vertical ledge—was performed by Mitch Kaufmann off the Tombstone in the 1977 East Coast Pro Tournament.

Top: *Aerial view of Kona Skatepark.* Inset: *Some of Kona's runs and features.* Photos by Erik Hamilton

a J-run, all of which remain today. Kona pioneered the vert ramp when it added the "Tombstone" to allow a vertical drop into the bowl. The vert ramp became a skatepark standard and led to the invention of the elevator drop, where a skater drops straight down off a vertical ledge.

Most early skateparks lasted only a few years, and Kona nearly shared that fate, going bankrupt and shutting down in early 1979. Six months later, Martin and Laurie Ramos stepped in. Though they had no previous experience in the skateboarding or amusement business, they hoped to keep the park going for their skater son Marty and kids like him. It has been a family affair ever since, with Marty Ramos taking over in 1996. In outlasting nearly every other early skatepark, it has become a bonafide historic site and a place of pilgrimage for three generations of skaters across the world.

COSMO AND THE GULLAH GEECHEE HERITAGE CORRIDOR

How much of Jacksonville's—and the South's—culture is owed to the Gullah Geechee people?

Thousands of Jaxsons can trace their ancestry to the Gullah Geechee, descendants of West Africans enslaved on the plantations of the Lowcountry, a coastal region stretching from Wilmington, North Carolina, to St. Augustine. In fact, though less famous than Charleston or Savannah, Jacksonville has the largest population of Gullah Geechee descendants in the country.

After the Civil War, many newly free Gullah Geechee from across the Lowcountry flocked to Jacksonville, a growing town with a large US military presence, for protection. Gullah Geechee culture and food became an intrinsic part of the city; dishes such as shrimp and grits, okra, seafood boil, and a Jacksonville specialty, garlic crabs (see page 42) remain popular today.

One of several communities established by Gullah Geechee settlers was Cosmo in present-day Arlington. Cosmo's founders carved out a life for themselves by farming, hunting, and fishing on Mill Cove. Centered around a 40-acre parcel granted to James Bartley in 1887, Cosmo had its own school, post office, and two churches. The churches historically practiced the ring shout, an

FREEDOM PARK, COSMO

WHAT: A city park dedicated to the history of the Gullah Geechee town of Cosmo

WHERE: 10946 Fort Caroline Rd.

COST: Free

PRO TIP: For more information on Gullah Geechee Heritage Corridor sites, visit gullahgeecheecorridor.org.

The Gullah Geechee community of Cosmo. Photo by Ennis Davis

ancient Gullah Geechee religious tradition in which participants stomp their feet in a counterclockwise circle.

By the 1950s, the community had declined due to pollution on the river and encroaching development, and it was gradually absorbed by sprawl on Fort Caroline Road. Still, many descendants of the founders feel a strong connection to Cosmo and its history. In 2020, the City of Jacksonville placed signs and historic markers around Cosmo and announced the creation of Freedom Park at the intersection of McCormick and Fort Caroline Roads to memorialize Cosmo and the Gullah Geechee people in general. It is part of the Gullah Geechee Heritage Corridor and is its most prominent Northeast Florida site so far.

Several of Cosmo's founders had been enslaved on the Kingsley Plantation across the river. For more information on the plantation, see page 80.

HONTOON OWL— THE WORLD'S LARGEST PRE-COLUMBIAN WOODCARVING

Who created the Hontoon Owl?

Part of the Timucuan Ecological and Historic Preserve, Fort Caroline National Memorial is best known for its replica of Fort Caroline, the settlement established in 1564 as a haven for French Huguenots. However, its visitor center also features an incredible and underappreciated Native American artifact. The Hontoon Owl is a 10-foot effigy carved from a single heart pine trunk around 1300 AD. It was found in the St. Johns River off Hontoon Island, an area inhabited by the Mayaca and Jororo peoples, who practiced a similar culture to the Timucua living to the north, but spoke their own language.

The owl was discovered accidentally in 1955 when landowner Victor Roepke was excavating for a residential development near Hontoon Island. Roepke pulled it ashore and called the Florida Museum in Gainesville to investigate. The finely detailed effigy was carved via burning the wood and scraping it down with a shark's-tooth or stone knife. The artist must have been a master woodcarver. It is the largest pre-Columbian wooden carving ever found in the Americas.

THE HONTOON OWL

WHAT: 10-foot Native American wood carving of an owl dating to around 1300 AD

WHERE: The Timucuan Preserve Visitor Center at 12751 Fort Caroline Rd.

COST: Free (donations are welcome at the visitor center)

PRO TIP: Be sure to also check out the Timucua canoe and other artifacts at the center.

The Hontoon Owl

The bottom of the pole was rotten, suggesting it had once stood on the bank before breaking and falling into the river, where it was preserved in the muck. It was found near the Thurston Midden archaeological site, which produced a number of other artifacts, including similar effigies of an otter and pelican. The Florida Museum preserved the owl and later transferred it to Fort Caroline.

The significance of the owl to its makers is unknown. It has been called a totem or clan animal, but scholars note owls were considered inauspicious, underworldly beings among the Timucua. Possibly the pole marked a burial place or charnel house. Whatever its import, the Hontoon Owl is an exquisite piece of Native American art, the like of which can't be found anywhere else.

Interestingly, the name of the Jororo or Hororo people living near Hontoon Island is the same as the Timucua word for owl, "hororo."

THE TIMUCUAN PRESERVE'S THEODORE ROOSEVELT AREA— THE GREATEST GIFT IN JACKSONVILLE HISTORY

Why did an eccentric hermit bequeath his land to the public?

William Henry "Willie" Browne III spent almost his entire life in the woods. His father, Jacksonville lawyer William Browne II, purchased 600 wild acres around the St. Johns Bluff in Arlington, and Willie and his brother Saxon remained on the land even after a house fire sent their parents back to the city. On Willie's 16th birthday in 1905, his father ceded him the entire property as both a gift and a charge, tasking him with defending it from those who would do it harm.

Willie spent the rest of his life living off his woods, protecting them from poachers and, worse, developers. As suburban sprawl overtook Arlington, Willie repeatedly rebuffed multimillion dollar offers for his land, saying simply, "money cannot buy happiness, and this place makes me happy." He and Saxon lived in a one-room cabin deep in the woods. Saxon's death in 1953 left Willie alone, and in 1969, he decided the land should become public space when he himself passed. Per his arrangement, on his death on December 14, 1970, the entire property transferred to the Nature Conservancy, with the stipulation that it forever be left natural. Today, Willie's woods are the Theodore Roosevelt Area, an intrinsic part of the Timucuan Ecological and Historic Preserve.

Thanks to Willie's gift, visitors can explore a slice of natural Florida, walking miles of trails through woods, marshlands, and a number of noteworthy spots. Some highlights include the family cemetery where Willie and kin lie, remains of an ancient Native American shell mound, the mysterious Round Marsh, and the foundations of Willie's

THE TIMUCUAN PRESERVE'S THEODORE ROOSEVELT AREA

WHAT: A 600-acre natural section of the Timucuan Preserve

WHERE: 13165 Mt. Pleasant Rd.

COST: Free

PRO TIP: An old Southern funerary custom is alive in the Theodore Roosevelt Area. Place a shell on Willie's grave (or any others) to show they're still remembered.

Top: *View of Round Marsh in the Theodore Roosevelt Area.* Inset: *Spearing grave on the shell midden.*

long destroyed cabin. Another unusual feature is a lone gravestone hidden beside the trail at the top of the bluff. It belongs to John Nathan Spearing, a shipyard owner and Confederate veteran who owned the property before the Brownes.

Willie Browne didn't want his woods to be named after him. Instead, he named them for Theodore Roosevelt, his ecological hero.

THE RIBAULT COLUMN

What became of the column left in Jacksonville by French explorer Jean Ribault?

In 1562, French explorer Jean Ribault became the first European to chart the St. Johns River. On a small island off the south bank, he erected a stone column emblazoned with the arms of King Charles IX, one of five he'd brought to claim the Southeast for France. He planted a second in South Carolina, but took the other three back to France.

In June 1564, Ribault's lieutenant René Goulaine de Laudonnière returned to Florida and established Fort Caroline on the St. Johns River. The French reported that Saturiwa, paramount chief of the local Mocama Timucua, and his son Athore invited them to visit Ribault's column. According to the French, the Mocama had made a shrine of it, decorating it with garlands and leaving offerings. Two surviving artworks depict this episode: a painting attributed to Fort Caroline's artist Jacques le Moyne and an engraving by Theodor de Bry, claimed to be based on le Moyne's work (see page 16).

The Spanish ejected the French from Florida in 1565. They located and removed the Parris Island column, but what became of the Florida version is unclear. In 1924, the Daughters of the American Revolution commissioned a replica based on de Bry's engraving. It initially stood at Mayport near the river's mouth and was moved to Mayport Road when Naval Station Mayport was

---

RIBAULT COLUMN

WHAT: 1924 replica of a lost column placed by French explorer Jean Ribault in 1562

WHERE: 13191 W Fort Caroline Park Rd.

COST: Free

PRO TIP: For more information on the French in Florida, check out Fort Caroline and its visitors center (see page 16).

The Ribault Column

built in 1940. In 1958, it was relocated to its present location, a dedicated riverside space in the Timucuan Ecological and Historic Preserve near the Fort Carolina replica and the Theodore Roosevelt Area (see page 152).

The story of Ribault's columns may not be over. In 2016, salvagers found a wreck identified as Ribault's lost ship *La Trinité*. On board was one of the columns. This incredible find opens the possibility that it could be displayed in the Timucuan Preserve in the future.

A number of things are named for Jean Ribault in Jacksonville, including Ribault High School, Fort George Island's Ribault Club, and the Ribault River.

SPANISH-AMERICAN WAR BATTERY

Why is there an old war fort in the middle of a suburban neighborhood?

A modest parcel on a quiet Arlington street is home to a piece of military history that was largely forgotten and neglected for more than 100 years. Though the Spanish-American War is one of America's less remembered conflicts, it had a major impact on Jacksonville, and a defensive battery atop the St. Johns Bluff stands as a physical reminder.

The battery was built in April 1898 at the outset of hostilities between the US and Spain, which primarily revolved around the issue of Cuban independence. As in much of Florida, support for Cuba was high in Jacksonville, St. Augustine, and Fernandina. In the 1890s, the region had a substantial Cuban population, much of which worked in the area's many Cuban cigar factories. With support from Jacksonville locals such as businessman José Huau, independence leader José Martí visited the city eight times, inspiring support among Cubans and non-Cubans alike. US-based interests attempted 73 missions to support the Cubans, of which 24 shipped from Jacksonville.

Jacksonville became a rallying point when the Spanish-American war began. The US 7th Army Corps established Camp Cuba Libre in Springfield as its headquarters. The St. Johns Bluff battery was intended to protect Jacksonville and the camp from

A historical marker in Springfield Park commemorates Camp Springfield, later Camp Cuba Libre, and the 7th Army Corps.

The Spanish American War Battery

SPANISH-AMERICAN WAR BATTERY

WHAT: Remains of an 1898 defensive battery

WHERE: Off Fort Caroline Road, near Huguenot Lane.

COST: Free

PRO TIP: A caveat to photographers: the site is not accessible to the public.

potential incursion by Spain. It was designed to house two 8-inch guns, but construction took longer than the war itself. The guns, never fired, were relocated and the space returned to private ownership, largely forgotten by the public.

The Timucuan Preserve long hoped to preserve the battery, but in 2017, a new owner bought the lot and planned to raze it. In 2018, the North Florida Land Trust raised funds to buy the land and transferred it to the National Parks Service, which plans to restore it as another feature of the Timucuan Preserve.

THE SALAAM CLUB AND THE RAMALLAH CLUB OF JACKSONVILLE

Where do Jacksonville's Arab American families celebrate their culture?

One thing that often surprises newcomers is that Jacksonville has America's 10th-largest Arab community and its 5th-largest Syrian community. For more than 130 years, Arab Americans have played an outsized role in the city in every conceivable field and area, including politics, business, health care, media, and the culinary scene.

Farris Mansour, a Lebanese fruit seller, became the first Arab to settle in Jacksonville around 1890. Hundreds more Arab immigrants followed over the next 30 years, attracted by Jacksonville's growing commercial sector and hospitable reputation for immigrants. Most early immigrants were Christians from Ottoman Syria, in particular present-day Lebanon, and most worked commercial jobs as grocers, shopkeepers, and small businesspeople. The fall of the Ottoman Empire in 1920 brought a second wave of Arab immigrants to Jacksonville, this time primarily Palestinians from the Christian city of Ramallah. Like the earlier immigrants, the newcomers entered the commercial sectors. Since the 1960s, an ongoing third wave has brought Middle Easterners from every country and background to Jacksonville, increasing the diversity of the community.

The Salaam Club and Ramallah Club of Jacksonville have been instrumental in the success of Jacksonville's vibrant Arab American community.

Top: *The Salaam Club.*
Bottom: *The Ramallah Club.*

SALAAM CLUB AND RAMALLAH CLUB OF JACKSONVILLE

WHAT: Social organizations founded by early Arab American families in Jacksonville

WHERE: Salaam Club: 8101 Beach Blvd.
Ramallah Club: 3130 Parental Home Rd.

COST: Free

PRO TIP: Both clubs host events for members.

The early immigrants immersed themselves quickly in wider Jacksonville society and found a substantially higher level of acceptance than in many other cities. Generations of Arab Americans have worked to preserve their culture and traditions. Social organizations and churches have been instrumental in this. The oldest organization, the Salaam Club, was founded in 1912 as the Syrian American Club. It later merged with two others, the Lebanon American Club and The Homs Brotherhood Club, and moved into its current five-acre location in 1959. Similarly, Palestinians founded the Ramallah Club of Jacksonville in 1953. Both clubs helped their members stay in touch, network, and assist more recent immigrants to Jacksonville. They both remain major forces in community life, hosting dances, weddings, dinners, and other events for members.

SEXY REXY, KING OF BEACH BOULEVARD

How did a concrete minigolf obstacle become a Jacksonville icon?

Like a shining light in the heathen darkness, one of Jacksonville's most famous landmarks keeps vigil from the front of a Beach Boulevard strip mall: Sexy Rexy, the orange concrete Tyrannosaurus.

Rexy started life around 1970 as an obstacle for a Goony Golf minigolf course. Founded in Chattanooga, Tennessee, in 1960, the chain had a second Jacksonville location on Blanding Boulevard. The tyrannosaurus and other whacky obstacles came from a stable of designs common to franchises across the country, but due to their immense size and weight, the concrete sculptures had to be built locally. In Jacksonville, Goony Golf hired Southeastern Pools owner Dick Calvert for his expertise in the materials.

The dinosaur that came to be known as Sexy Rexy is 20 feet tall and painted orange. His left arm clutches a bone for stability. Originally, his right arm raised and lowered a caveman for players to putt under. Due to his striking appearance and location close to Beach Boulevard, he quickly became a popular landmark for travelers. He's one of several Goony Golf statues still in existence across the US.

Goony Golf closed in 1999 and was sold in 2001 to Ash Properties, who planned to replace it with a strip mall. Much of the attraction was razed, but Rexy was spared. Still, a wave of anxiety swept

SEXY REXY

WHAT: A concrete tyrannosaurus that once ruled a minigolf course and somehow became one of the city's most recognizable landmarks

WHERE: 10150 Beach Blvd.

COST: Free

PRO TIP: Have you even *been* to Jacksonville if you don't get a picture of Sexy Rexy?

Sexy Rexy in all his glory

Jacksonville that he might be removed. Ash fielded purchase offers from across the nation, and the City of Jacksonville offered to move him downtown.

In the end, community pleas and the difficulty of moving something so heavy led Ash to announce that Sexy Rexy would stay put as a mascot for the shopping center. In 2007, Ash brought in a team of University of North Florida construction students to repair him, restoring an appearance befitting a king.

Another former roadside statue stands at Downtown's Metropolitan Park. A 22-foot alligator from the erstwhile Gatorland attraction in St. Johns County was moved here when it closed in 1982.

MUSSALLEM GALLERIES: RUGS, FINE ART, AND ANTIQUITIES

Where can you see—and buy—the works of master artists?

One of Jacksonville's best kept secrets stands in a huge showroom building on Philips Highway. Featuring a collection of art, Oriental rugs, antiques, and other valuables, Mussallem Galleries is the biggest privately owned gallery in North Florida and one of the biggest anywhere.

Passed down through five generations of the Mussallem clan, Mussallem Galleries is almost certainly the oldest family-owned business in Jacksonville. It started all the way back in 1897, when the Mussallem family came to St. Augustine from Zahle, Lebanon, part of the first wave of Arab immigrants to Northeast Florida (see page 158). Charles Mussallem Sr., then just 13, started selling fine rugs to wealthy residents and visitors and built up a lucrative business. By 1912, his company had outgrown the town, and he relocated north to Downtown Jacksonville.

His son Charles Mussallem Jr. expanded the business even further, founding related companies that clean rugs and make padding to go under them. He also expanded the offerings to include antique furniture and decorations. The expansion required a much larger building, so the gallery built its 90,000 square foot warehouse on Philips Highway. The building's exterior doesn't do justice to what's inside. As Mussallem Jr. told visitors, "We

(see page 158)

MUSSALLEM GALLERIES

WHAT: Massive art gallery

WHERE: 5801 Philips Hwy., Ste. A

COST: Free to visit and peruse

PRO TIP: Art lovers should also check out Jacksonville's museums: the Cummer Museum and MOCA Jacksonville.

Mussallem Galleries main room. Photo courtesy of the Mussallem Galleries

built it to have all the character of a fine museum, but with one difference: we have a price tag on all our pieces."

Charles Jr.'s sons Charles III and James built on the gallery's museum identity by acquiring paintings and other artworks. Today, the gallery has more than 4,000 paintings, 1,000 rugs, and hundreds of vases, sculptures, and other objets d'art. Among the masters represented at Mussallem Galleries are Vincent Van Gogh, Rembrandt, Marc Chagall, and Pablo Picasso.

Mussallem Galleries has donated many paintings to local schools, universities, and museums, where they can be seen today.

HARRIET BEECHER STOWE'S MANDARIN SCHOOL

What brought a famed abolitionist to Jacksonville?

Harriet Beecher Stowe galvanized the antislavery movement with her 1851 novel *Uncle Tom's Cabin* and after the Civil War, she decided to put her abolitionism into practice. She fell in love with Northeast Florida during a visit in 1866, and the next year, she purchased a winter home on the St. Johns River in Mandarin, then a small agricultural community, to take an active role in Reconstruction.

For the next 18 years, Stowe and her family spent winters in Mandarin. There Stowe wrote some of her most notable later works, including *Palmetto Leaves*, the first significant promotional work about Florida. The freedmen and women Stowe met in Mandarin believed that education was key to improving their lives and providing new opportunities, so Stowe purchased a lot near her cottage and convinced the Freedmen's Bureau to establish a Mandarin branch and school. In 1869, the Bureau completed the first Mandarin School, which served Black citizens and White alike and doubled as a community center. Stowe's husband Calvin Stowe hosted church services in the building on Sundays, and other family members provided music and lessons.

The original Mandarin School building burned down under unclear circumstances in fall 1872. Stowe was devastated, and personally raised money from across the country to rebuild. The

For more info on the Mandarin Community Club, visit mandarincommunityclub.org. Up the street, the Mandarin Museum also has exhibits on Stowe and other aspects of Mandarin history.

Mandarin Community Club, formerly the Mandarin School

MANDARIN COMMUNITY CLUB

WHAT: Community center and former integrated school

WHERE: 12447 Mandarin Rd.

COST: Free to visit, but the building can be rented

PRO TIP: Historical markers here and at the site of the Stowe cottage tell the story of her time in Mandarin.

new building opened the next year. Stowe would continue wintering in Mandarin until 1884, when her age made travel impossible.

With the end of Reconstruction and the onset of Jim Crow, the Mandarin School became segregated, but it continued serving local students until 1929. In 1936, the building was acquired by the Mandarin Community Club, a civic organization that still owns it today. Part of a cluster of buildings that offer a look at Mandarin's long-gone rural past, it stands as a tribute to Stowe's legacy in Northeast Florida.

THE BRUMOS COLLECTION

Where can you see one of the world's biggest collections of vintage endurance racecars?

In 1953, Hubert Brundage founded a Volkswagen shop, Brundage Motors, in Miami Springs, in large part to finance his interest in endurance racing. He moved to Jacksonville in 1955 and opened up shop on Main Street in Springfield. In 1959, he also began selling his preferred racecars, Porsches, and shortened the name to Brumos.

In 1960, Brundage founded his own formal endurance racing team, Brumos Racing, to compete on the world stage. The team's early success, including a second-place finish at the 12 Hours of Sebring in 1960, was cut short when Brundage died in a car accident in 1964. Brundage's friend, racecar driver Peter Gregg, purchased the dealership and racing team to keep Brundage's dream alive. Under Gregg and fellow driver Hurley Haywood, the team became one of the premier endurance racing organizations, racking up victories in the sport's Triple Crown, including five wins at the 24 Hours of Daytona, two in the 12 Hours of Sebring, and three at the 24 Hours of Le Mans.

Gregg's wife Elizabeth ran the organization after his death in 1980, and Dano Davis and Bob Snodgrass took over in 1990. Brumos Racing saw further successes, including 12 more wins at the 24 Hours of Daytona from 1994 to 2012. Throughout this time, the racecars were kept in a warehouse adjacent to Brumos

THE BRUMOS COLLECTION

WHAT: Endurance racecar museum

WHERE: 5159 San Pablo Rd. S.

COST: $25 for adults

PRO TIP: Check out the Porsche 917K from the 1970 Steve McQueen movie *Le Mans*.

Brumos Racing's collection of historic Porsche racecars

Mercedes-Benz on Atlantic Boulevard and periodically displayed at the dealerships. Davis sold the business in 2015.

To display the vast racecar collection and celebrate Brumos Racing's legacy, Davis established the Brumos Collection off San Pablo Road. Part of the museum is dedicated to Brumos's Porsches, including those used in historic races. Another section features historic automobiles from Davis's private collection. One of the biggest endurance racing museums in the Southeast, it's a must-see for any car lover.

Brumos raced under the number 59. Peter Gregg, a former naval intelligence officer, took it from the hull number of the ship he served on, the USS *Forrestal*, CV-59.

BEACHES MUSEUM

What did the Jacksonville Beaches look like before the high rises and nightlife?

The Jacksonville Beaches are a chain of communities on the north end of a nameless barrier island south of the St. Johns River mouth. Jacksonville Beach, Neptune Beach, and Atlantic Beach are three cities that kept their own governments when Jacksonville consolidated with Duval County in 1968. Mayport is part of the City of Jacksonville (see page 174), while Ponte Vedra Beach and Palm Valley are in neighboring St. Johns County.

The Beaches have a long history. The current communities emerged in the 19th and early 20th centuries, with oceanfront resorts being major drivers. They are now among Northeast Florida's most popular areas, and the communities are a regional draw for recreation and nightlife. Unfortunately, this popularity has come at the price of the loss of an increasing number of historic homes and buildings.

BEACHES MUSEUM

WHAT: Museum dedicated to Jacksonville Beaches history

WHERE: 381 Beach Blvd., Jacksonville Beach

COST: Free

PRO TIP: The museum offers guided tours from the main office.

The Beaches' island is unnamed because it didn't become an island until 1912, when the Intracoastal Waterway connected the San Pablo and Tolomato inlets. Some call it San Pablo Island.

The Oesterreicher-McCormick Cabin at the Beaches Museum

Fortunately for those waxing nostalgic over earlier times on the island, the Beaches Museum has taken in some old buildings that would otherwise be lost. Buildings relocated to the history park include the 1903 Pablo Beach Post Office (Pablo Beach was an earlier name of Jacksonville Beach) and the 1887 Beaches Chapel, the Beaches' first church. There's also the old Mayport railroad depot and a historic train engine.

Perhaps the most interesting building at the museum is the Oesterreicher-McCormick Cabin. This Florida cracker-style cabin was built by Thomas Oesterreicher in 1873 in Palm Valley, then an isolated rural backwood. The Oesterreichers made their living by farming, raising cattle, and harvesting palmetto fronds for Palm Sunday celebrations. The cabin remained in the same family until 2016, when Thomas Oesterreicher's great-granddaughter transferred it to the Beaches Museum, where it was restored.

THE JACKSONVILLE BEACH PIER AND THE BIRTH OF FIRST COAST SURFING

How did a fishing pier introduce a city to one of its favorite sports?

The Jacksonville Beach Pier is a popular place for fisherfolk, sightseers, and, of course, surfers. Less appreciated is the fact that the pier, or rather an earlier incarnation of it, played an instrumental role in surfing taking off in the First Coast during the "Endless Summer" of 1964.

Jacksonville Beach's first pier opened in 1922 at Second Avenue North. By the 1960s, it was showing its age, and some city council members wanted it gone. In 1962, the pier burned down mysteriously as the city debated its future. The town would have gone without a pier if businessman R. L. Williams hadn't built one himself at Sixth Avenue South the following year.

As strange as it seems now, surfing was nearly unknown in Northeast Florida at the time. A few locals had been paddling out since the 1930s, but as late as 1962, there were only a handful of regulars in the Jacksonville Beaches. The 1963 pier changed that dramatically. It created breaks on both sides that could be surfed even at high tide when other breaks were flat. It also provided a

The explosion of surfing in Jacksonville led to interest in skateboarding in the 1970s and the birth of the city's historic Kona Skatepark (see page 146).

The Jacksonville Beach Pier. Photo by Paul Brennan

place for surfers to congregate and show off. Then the next year, the pier drew an event that changed First Coast surfing forever.

On July 9, filmmaker Bruce Brown rolled into town on a roadshow for his legendary surfing film *The Endless Summer*. He started with a demonstration by star surfers at the pier and screened the movie that night. The events drew thousands and caused a surfing fever that hasn't broken since.

JACKSONVILLE BEACH PIER

WHAT: A public pier

WHERE: 503 1st St. N, Jacksonville Beach

COST: $3 for fishing and $1 for sightseeing

PRO TIP: Visit in May when the pier hosts the Wavemasters Surf Contest.

The Sixth Avenue pier was ravaged by Hurricane Floyd in 1999, and the City of Jacksonville replaced it with a sturdier new pier at Fifth Avenue North in 2004. Located in Jacksonville Beach's business district, the current pier is an even more popular surfing hot spot than its predecessor.

ALPHA PAYNTER, GHOST OF TacoLu

Does the spirit of a 20th-century businesswoman haunt a popular Jacksonville Beach taco joint?

Tex-Mex restaurant TacoLu, which occupies the rustic former Homestead Restaurant building in Jacksonville Beach, has a reputation as one of the most haunted places in Jacksonville. According to local tradition, original owner Alpha Paynter never left.

Paynter was a prominent Jacksonville Beach businesswoman for decades, although parts of her background are a mystery. No photograph of her has been found, and her maiden name is unknown. What is known is that she was born in 1887 and came to Jacksonville in the 1920s. She moved to Jacksonville Beach after divorcing her husband in 1930 and opened her first restaurant, the Copper Kettle.

In 1934, Paynter originally built the log cabin that would become the Homestead as a boarding house. In 1947, she made it into a family-style restaurant specializing in her own Southern cooking. She sold the Homestead in 1961 and died the next year; it continued under a succession of owners for another 50 years. It closed for good in 2011, and the next year, the building was taken over by TacoLu. The new owners kept the homey architecture but added Mexican-inspired decorations and murals.

TacoLu is an example of old Jacksonville Beaches architecture that has survived into the present era. For a deeper dive into how the Beaches once looked, visit the Beaches Museum.

TacoLu, the former Homestead Restaurant

The Homestead's log cabin aesthetic and decades-long role in Beaches culture made it ripe for ghost stories, and claims that the Homestead is haunted spread shortly after Paynter's death. While several different ghosts and legends have been reported, true to her name, Alpha is the undisputed leader. She's generally said to be a benevolent spirit seen near the fireplace, on the stairs, or in the women's bathroom.

The TacoLu staff are just as diligent as those at the old Homestead about noting and sharing ghost sightings and stories about Paynter, so it's likely the old building's reputation as a famous haunted place will remain intact for years to come.

TACOLU, FORMERLY THE HOMESTEAD

WHAT: A taco restaurant in an old log cabin said to be haunted by its builder, businesswoman Alpha Paynter

WHERE: 1712 Beach Blvd., Jacksonville Beach

COST: The price of a taco or drink

PRO TIP: Alpha Paynter's ghost is most commonly reported by the fireplace in the main dining room.

MAYPORT VILLAGE

What are Mayport shrimp, anyway?

Mayport may have seen better days, but it's still worth a visit as an authentic Old Florida fishing community with an intriguing history and some unusual sites to see. It's also one of the best places to get fresh seafood in a city known for it.

Located where the Intracoastal Waterway flows into the St. Johns River and spitting distance from the Atlantic Ocean, Mayport has always been a strategic location. Explorer Jean Ribault planted a column claiming Florida for France near Mayport in 1562 (see page 154). In the early 19th century, it was home to a small colony of fishermen and river pilots; a town was formally laid out in 1847. In 1940, the US Navy acquired much of the land for Naval Station Mayport, leaving Mayport Village as a residential neighborhood and working waterfront.

In the early 20th century, Mayport fishermen adopted innovations introduced in nearby Fernandina (see page 110) to help revolutionize the shrimping industry. Mayport grew into a significant shrimping port; "Mayport shrimp" became a byword across the Jacksonville area for fresh local shrimp. Mayport shrimp aren't some special kind of shrimp; they're simply shrimp caught wild along the Southeastern coast and sold in Mayport. The distinction is significant today as the market is flooded with factory-farmed imports.

Though Mayport's fishing industry has declined since the 1990s, it remains Jacksonville's fresh seafood nexus. Key spaces include docks for fishing boats, Singleton's Seafood Shack, and Safe Harbor Seafood,

> ### MAYPORT VILLAGE
>
> **WHAT:** Historic fishing community
>
> **WHERE:** The northern end of A1A
>
> **COST:** Free
>
> **PRO TIP:** Safe Harbor Seafood is about the best place in the First Coast to get fresh shrimp and fish.

Top: *Safe Harbor Seafood in Mayport.*
Inset: *The old St. Johns River Lighthouse.*

which features a restaurant, market, and the area's only remaining seafood distribution operation. Other points of interest include the St. Johns River Ferry, which runs between Mayport and the Northside, the historic former Old St. Johns River Lighthouse, and the King House, a historic building reputed to be haunted by dozens of ghosts.

The City of Jacksonville's long-term plans include rebuilding Mayport's docks and strengthening the local shrimping and fishing industries.

BELUTHAHATCHEE: STETSON KENNEDY'S HOME

Where can you visit the home of renowned author Stetson Kennedy?

Tucked away off State Road 13 in St. Johns County is the homestead of author, folklorist, and human rights champion Stetson Kennedy. One of the most unique personalities ever to come from Jacksonville, he is remembered as the writer whose pen dealt a mortal blow to the Ku Klux Klan.

In 1937, the young Kennedy joined the Works Progress Administration's Florida Writers Project as supervisor over folklore. The project's headquarters were in Downtown Jacksonville, with the offices for African Americans at the Clara White Mission (see page 26). Among the staff was author Zora Neale Hurston (see page 36). In 1939, the project published *Florida: A Guide to the Southernmost State*, and after the war, Kennedy adapted unused material into *Palmetto Country*, a highly regarded "barefoot social history of Florida."

Kept from serving in World War II by a back injury, Kennedy declared war on a domestic enemy: the Klan. He infiltrated the organization and funneled its secrets to the authorities, the media, and even Superman—thanks to Kennedy, the Man of Steel battled the Klan on his radio show. In 1954, Kennedy published *The Klan Unmasked*, which revealed and ridiculed the Klan's rituals and code words. The theretofore powerful organization never recovered.

The Stetson Kennedy Foundation keeps the legacy of Stetson Kennedy, Woody Guthrie, and Beluthahatchee alive. For more information or to schedule a tour, visit stetsonkennedy.com.

Beluthahatchee, former home of author Stetson Kennedy

BELUTHAHATCHEE PARK

WHAT: Homesite of Stetson Kennedy

WHERE: 1501 State Route 13 N, Fruit Cove

COST: Free

PRO TIP: The grounds are open daily, but you can schedule a guided tour to go inside the buildings.

In 1948, Kennedy established Beluthahatchee, a lakeside residential development with protected woodlands. The name comes from a mythical land in African American folklore as recorded by Hurston, who described Beluthahatchee as "a Florida Shangri-La, where all unpleasant doings and sayings are forgotten." Kennedy maintained a home here that became a retreat for writers and artists. Folk singer Woody Guthrie was a regular guest; while there he wrote 80 songs and his autobiography, *Seeds of Man*. After Kennedy's death in 2011, the county turned the five acres around his house into Beluthahatchee Park.

ST. JOHNS COUNTY'S GHOST LIGHT ROAD

What caused the mysterious light on Greenbriar Road?

From the 1960s until 2001, a quiet, unpaved St. Johns County road was a major destination for local thrill-seekers. At night, Greenbriar Road was haunted by the "ghost light," an eerie light that seemed to follow cars before suddenly vanishing. As one of those thrill-seekers, I can personally testify that the ghost light was a real phenomenon; my friends and I saw it numerous times from 1997 to 2001.

Like any good haunted place, the light had an explanatory legend. As the story goes, a young motorcyclist got cocky and lost his head in a horrific accident on Greenbriar, and his ghost took up a nightly patrol. Apocryphal story aside, sightings were so prolific that the county sheriff investigated in 1987 but came to no firm conclusion. Explanations have ranged from supernatural forces to swamp gas to drugrunners' signals, but one mundane theory seems most plausible.

Greenbriar Road developed from the 18th-century Fatio Road, which connected Francis Fatio's New Switzerland Plantation to the King's Road. When County Road 210 was established, it followed part of the old Fatio Road before doglegging southwest at the current intersection with Greenbriar Road. This created a situation

---

GHOST LIGHT ROAD (GREENBRIAR ROAD)

WHAT: A quiet road where a strange phenomenon, the "ghost light," was seen for decades

WHERE: Greenbriar Road, between State Rd. 13 and County Rd. 210

COST: Free

PRO TIP: There's not much to see here today, but while you're in the area stop by Alpine Groves Park on State Road 13 to see how St. Johns County looked in its agricultural days.

By night, Greenbriar Road became the "Ghost Light Road."

where westbound 210 curved left at Greenbriar instead of meeting it straightaway. This may have created an optical illusion in which headlights appeared to come up Greenbriar—at such a distance that two lights looked like one—before banking through the intersection and disappearing.

Supporting this theory is the fact that after the intersection was redesigned for safety in 2001, the ghost light was never seen again. The road is now a paved suburban arterial with none of its old bucolic mystique. Nonetheless, for the old thrill-seekers, Greenbriar will forever be the Ghost Light Road.

Greenbriar Road is also known as Airport Road or Bombing Range Road after an abandoned naval airfield located there in the 1940s. Traces of runways can still be seen today.

DATIL PEPPERS

Did you know the First Coast grows its own breed of incredibly hot pepper?

Many farms, gardens, and front porches across the First Coast grow a crop that's become a local legend: the datil pepper. These small, exceptionally hot peppers, gold or orange when ripe, are pervasive in local restaurants and recipes. However, many locals don't realize they're basically unknown elsewhere. That's a shame, because not only are they delicious, they've got a fascinating history.

Two rival origin myths attribute the arrival of the datil pepper in St. Augustine to different groups with centuries of history in the First Coast: the Cubans and Minorcans. Minorcans, from the Spanish Mediterranean island of Menorca, came to Florida to settle the New Smyrna colony in the 18th century. When this failed, they relocated to St. Augustine, where their descendants number about 25,000 today. Datil peppers have long been part of local Minorcan cuisine, lending credence to the story that they brought them over.

However, the pepper plant is native to the Americas and isn't grown in Minorca. The datil pepper is a variety of the *Capsicum chinense*, or habanero-type pepper, which comes from the Caribbean and Central America; "habanero" refers to Havana, Cuba. Florida's Cuban connection dates to the earliest days of Spanish colonization in the 16th century and continues today, providing an easy method of transmission for the datil pepper.

DATIL PEPPER FESTIVAL

WHAT: An annual celebration of the datil pepper

WHERE: Held at the St. Johns County Agricultural Center generally on the first weekend in October. Outside the festival, datil peppers, plants, and products can be found at many stores, restaurants, and nurseries.

COST: Free

PRO TIP: Try datil pepper hot sauces from local companies such as Dat'l Do-It, Minorcan Mike's, and Minorcan Datil Pepper Products.

Left: *Datil peppers growing on a Jacksonville front porch.*
Inset: *A pepper*

Further cementing the Cuban origin theory is a 1937 *St. Augustine Record* article that reveals datils were first brought to St. Augustine from Santiago, Cuba, by local jelly maker Esteban B. Valls around 1880. Valls's peppers thrived and quickly became popular around town, with the Minorcans embracing them as their own.

Today, datil peppers are found throughout the First Coast in dishes, sauces, and marinades. The University of Florida's St. Johns County IFAS Extension hosts an annual Datil Pepper Festival each fall.

Dátil means "date" (as in the fruit of a date palm) in both Spanish and the Catalan language of Menorca.

CASTLE OTTTIS

Why is there a castle in Vilano Beach—and why does its name have three T's?

Towering over the live oaks and coastal scrub off A1A north of Vilano Beach is a sight that often causes uninitiated travelers to do a double take: a medieval European castle. This is Castle Otttis—and yes, it's really spelled that way.

The structure was built between 1984 and 1988 by Rusty Ickes and Ottis Sadler, a stonemason, on Ickes' back property. The two built the entire structure themselves, without plans or blueprints. Their only motivation was a desire to create a work of art to honor God.

Architecturally, the building is a folly, a structure not built for habitation or use but rather for aesthetic purposes. Composed of split-face concrete block, its design is inspired by medieval Irish castles. It has no electricity or plumbing, or glass on its 88 windows, and officially it's classified as a garage.

Ickes was so thrilled by the finished castle that he named it after Sadler. The third "T" came from an early misspelling that Ickes decided to keep as it recalled the three crosses at calvary where Jesus died.

At the suggestion of a local priest, Ickes had the interior fashioned after a medieval abbey chapel. Built by woodworker Lee Carpenter from 1988 to 1991, the trappings include eight carved staircases, an altar, a pulpit, pews, and a choir. As the windows are open to the elements, Carpenter used mostly water-resistant cypress.

CASTLE OTTTIS

WHAT: A replica castle

WHERE: 103 3rd St., St. Augustine

COST: Free (to see from the street)

PRO TIP: The best view of the castle is near the corner of 3rd Street and A1A.

View of the castle

Ickes never sought out publicity for his castle, but it was so conspicuous and so unusual—even by St. Augustine standards—that visitors flocked to it anyway. Eventually Ickes opened it to the public for a Christian church service and tours. It has also hosted weddings, photo shoots, and events, not to mention many a curious passerby wondering why there's a castle in the quiet coastal scrubland of Vilano Beach.

Castle Otttis is open for monthly Christian church services or by appointment. To see the interior for yourself, schedule a tour at castleotttis.com.

SECRETS OF THE FOUNTAIN OF YOUTH

Is a St. Augustine tourist attraction the location of a secret treasure?

The Fountain of Youth is the most enduring legend associated with Florida. According to the story, conquistador Juan Ponce de Leon was searching for its youth-restoring waters when he came to Florida in 1513. The Fountain is an ancient myth that only became attached to Ponce years after his death, but it has captured the imagination of visitors to Florida for centuries. By the 1870s, the well at what's now St. Augustine's Fountain of Youth Archaeological Park was promoted as the "real" Fountain, one of dozens of wells and springs making that claim throughout the state.

Fountain of Youth Park may not have magical waters, but it's an important archaeological and historic site. Its grounds are the location of the Timucua town of Seloy and the original site of the St. Augustine colony from 1565. The park is also one of Florida's oldest tourist attractions, continuously operated since 1903.

The old park may still have secrets to share. It's considered the most likely location of a secret treasure, buried in the ancient year of 1982. Publisher Byron Priess covertly buried 12 casques in North American cities, each holding a key to a safety deposit box that contained a valuable jewel. He then published a book, *The Secret:*

FOUNTAIN OF YOUTH ARCHAEOLOGICAL PARK

WHAT: Tourist attraction

WHERE: 11 Magnolia Ave., St. Augustine

COST: $15.96 for adults, $15.02 for seniors and $8.45 for kids

PRO TIP: You can take a drink from the well. Don't get your hopes up about renewed youth.

Entrance to the Fountain of Youth Archaeological Park

A Treasure Hunt, which featured 12 mysterious paintings and 12 opaque verses containing clues as to the treasures' locations. To date, only three casques have been found. Only Priess knew the locations, and he took them to his grave when he died in 2005.

Treasure hunters believe the clues, including a painting featuring a conquistador, point to one cache being in St. Augustine, specifically at or near the Fountain of Youth. If the treasure is at the Fountain of Youth, it may be lost for good. The discovery of the important archaeological sites in the 1990s means that digging for treasure is off limits, so this is one secret that may never be revealed.

A community of treasure hunters dedicated to discovering Preiss's secret treasures has an informative and very thorough website. Check out their interpretations of the St. Augustine clues here: thesecret.pbworks.com.

THE HURRICANE LADY

Does a saintly statue protect St. Augustine from hurricanes?

Though it has taken considerable storm damage, the First Coast has suffered few direct hits by hurricanes. Climatologists attribute this to blind luck, but some locals think divine intervention may play a part. According to tradition, a saintly statue called the Hurricane Lady has delivered St. Augustine from storms since 1850.

The story goes that a Spanish ship headed for St. Augustine was beset by a storm. The captain ordered everything not battened down thrown overboard. Finally, the sailors came across an unlabeled crate containing a statue of a saint. The crew knelt down and prayed for her intercession, and the captain vowed he'd give the statue to the first Christian family they encountered if they survived. Miraculously, the storm abated, and when the ship reached port, the captain gifted the statue to the Rodrigues family.

The Rodrigueses were part of St. Augustine's Minorcan community, descendants of laborers from the Spanish island of

THE HURRICANE LADY AT THE FATHER MIGUEL O'REILLY HOUSE MUSEUM

WHAT: Saint's statue

WHERE: 32 Aviles St., St. Augustine

COST: Free (donations are welcome)

PRO TIP: Another revered statue of the Virgin Mary is nearby at the Shrine of Our Lady of La Leche.

The Sisters of St. Joseph came to Florida from France on a mission to educate newly freed African Americans after the Civil War. They're still heavily involved in education today.

Top: *The Father Miguel O'Reilly House Museum.* Inset: *The Hurricane Lady.*

Menorca (see page 180). Minorcan families maintained the tradition of praying to the Hurricane Lady during hurricane season down the generations, and the statue passed to the Benet family, who maintained a shrine in their house. In the 1980s, the Benets gave the statue to the Sisters of St. Joseph, a congregation of nuns founded in 1866. Since 2003, the sisters have displayed the statue at the Father Miguel O'Reilly House Museum, St. Augustine's oldest home.

There's some disagreement about the identity of the Hurricane Lady. The sisters consider her an image of the Virgin Mary. However, looking at some of her accoutrements, others think she's actually Santa Barbara. All agree, however, that she's a protective force for believers in the ancient city, who still draws worshipers every hurricane season.

FORT MOSE

Where was the first free Black town in the US?

St. Augustine is the oldest continuously inhabited, European-settled community in the continental US, but it still has secrets and hidden histories waiting to be found. One site has revealed much about a forgotten side of St. Augustine since its rediscovery in 1968: Fort Mose, site of the first free Black town in the modern US.

In 1689, Spanish Florida began offering amnesty to escapees from British plantations in Georgia and Carolina in an effort to build up defenses and to undermine the British colonies' plantation economies. The freedom seekers were required to adopt Catholicism, join the militia, and protect St. Augustine in case of an invasion. As Florida's free Black population grew, Governor Manuel de Montiano established Gracia Real de Santa Teresa de Mose in 1738 as a free Black settlement and bulwark against the British.

Fort Mose quickly became a haven for free Blacks and freedom seekers from the British colonies. At its peak, it had high wooden palisades, a population of about 100, and its own church. It was abandoned in 1763 when Spain transferred Florida to Great Britain; most inhabitants left for Cuba or Florida's Seminole towns, joining the Black Seminole population.

The British cracked down on the free Black population, and for more than two centuries, Fort Mose was forgotten, its location lost. In 1968, St. Augustine museum owner Jack Williams pored over old maps and became convinced a salt marsh north of town

FORT MOSE HISTORIC STATE PARK

WHAT: Site of the Spanish Fort Mose, the first free Black settlement in the present-day US

WHERE: 15 Fort Mose Trail, St. Augustine

COST: Park admission is free; visitor center is $2 per person (kids under 6 are free).

PRO TIP: The boardwalk is a great place for bird-watching or simply getting away.

Top: *The location of Fort Mose today.* Inset: *Fort Mose visitors center.*

contained the remnants of Fort Mose. To save the land from pending development, he bought it himself and began excavating. Though his theory was initially dismissed, over time, archaeology proved him right. Following an acrimonious legal battle, the State of Florida acquired the location for a state park. It includes a museum, boardwalk, and reenactors telling the story of American's first free Black settlement.

Fort Mose Historic State Park is considered the premier site on the Florida Black Heritage Trail, which has 43 sites across the Jacksonville area.

MARINELAND

Where is the world's first oceanarium?

Decades before SeaWorld became Florida's go-to place to see captive marine mammals put on shows, Marineland was one of the state's top tourist attractions, drawing 900,000 visitors a year. Though much has changed since its heyday, this park straddling the border of Flagler and St. Johns Counties on A1A was the world's first oceanarium and the first park featuring dolphins and whales.

The park began as Marine Studios in 1938, and the owners initially envisioned it as a place where sea creatures could be studied and filmed in captivity. Some movies were filmed there over the years, including *Creature from the Black Lagoon* in 1954 and its sequel *Revenge of the Creature* in 1955, but almost immediately, the park's draw as a tourist attraction outweighed its success as a filming location, especially after the staff learned that dolphins could be trained to do tricks. It initially consisted of two large tanks exhibiting the animals as well as dolphin and sea lion shows. The name was later changed to Marineland, and the park expanded over the next few decades, with additions including a "Porpoise Stadium," motel, restaurants, bars, and a campground.

Marineland saw an increase in visitors when Disney World opened near Orlando in 1971 and brought even more tourists to Florida. However, when SeaWorld opened two years later, it competed directly with the much smaller Marineland. The park

---

MARINELAND DOLPHIN ADVENTURE

WHAT: World's oldest oceanarium

WHERE: 9600 N. Ocean Shore Blvd., Marineland

COST: General admission is $15 for adults, $8 for kids, and $14 for seniors; dolphin encounters are purchased separately.

PRO TIP: You can also tour the University of Florida's nearby Whitney Laboratory for Marine Bioscience.

A dolphin show at Marineland

entered a period of decline, which was eventually compounded by changing attitudes about marine mammals in captivity. From the 1980s, Marineland passed through a succession of owners, none of whom could recapture its earlier success. A renovation in 2006 razed many of the original features, including the two main tanks. In 2011, the park was purchased by the Georgia Aquarium and converted into Marineland Dolphin Adventure, which focuses on dolphin swims.

Marineland is also the name of the town surrounding the park. The town and Flagler County own much of the historic park property as the River to Sea Preserve.

SOURCES

The Great Fire of 1901—Jacksonville's Greatest Tragedy: Foley, Bill, and Wayne W. Wood. The Great Fire of 1901. Jacksonville Historical Society, 2001.

DUUUVAL!: Field, Mike. "Black History Celebrated in Public Art." TheJaxsonMag.com, July 15, 2019. thejaxsonmag.com/article/black-history-celebrated-in-public-art

St. John's Cathedral: Strange Roads and Poltergeists: Davis, Ennis. "Sites & Scenes: The Cathedral District." TheJaxsonMag.com, March 30, 2021. thejaxsonmag.com/article/sites-scenes-the-cathedral-district; Gilmore, Tim. "Cathedral District: The Bodies in Billy Goat Hill." TheJaxsonMag.com, April 8, 2021. thejaxsonmag.com/article/cathedral-district-the-bodies-in-billy-goat-hill

Chamblin's, a Booklover's Labyrinth: Patton, Charlie. "Four Decades Later, Ron Chamblin Keeps Selling, Buying Books." *The Florida Times-Union*, July 19, 2016. jacksonville.com/entertainment/arts/2016-07-19/story/four-decades-later-ron-chamblin-keeps-selling-buying-books

Duval Bass: The Miami Bass Sound in Jacksonville: Field, Mike. "Public Art Sparks Jax Music History Lessons." TheJaxsonMag.com, June 21, 2019. thejaxsonmag.com/article/public-art-sparks-jax-music-history-lessons

The Train Buried beneath a Skyscraper: Field, Mike. "A Locomotive Is Buried below This Skyscraper." TheJaxsonMag.com, January 8, 2017. thejaxsonmag.com/article/a-locomotive-is-buried-below-this-skyscraper

Downtown's Underground Tunnels: Davis, Ennis. "The Hidden Tunnels of Union Terminal." TheJaxsonMag.com, June 10, 2019. thejaxsonmag.com/article/the-hidden-tunnels-of-union-terminal; Hull, Shelton. "Touring Downtown's Network of Tunnels." *The Florida Times-Union*, December 8, 2019. jacksonville.com/opinion/20191208/touring-downtowns-network-of-tunnels

Fort Caroline Engravings at the Jacksonville Main Library: Le Moyne-de Bry Engravings from the Ansbacher Map Collection. JaxPublicLibrary.com, 2021. jaxpubliclibrary.org/research/collections/le-moyne-de-bry-engravings-ansbacher-map-collection; Milanich, Jerald T. "The Devil in the Details." *Archaeology*, May/June 2005. archive.archaeology.org/0505/abstracts/florida.html

Ossachite: A Lost Timucua City? Delaney, Bill. "Ossachite: A Lost Timucua City?" TheJaxsonMag.com, forthcoming.

LaVilla, the Harlem of the South: Davis, Ennis. "LaVilla of the North: Harlem." MetroJacksonville.com, April 2, 2015. metrojacksonville.com/article/2015-apr-lavilla-of-the-north-harlem; Davis, Ennis. "The Remains of Jax's Ragtime, Blues and Jazz Age." ModernCities.com, December 4, 2017. moderncities.com/article/2017-dec-the-remains-of-jaxs-ragtime-blues-and-jazz-age; Davis, Ennis. "Ma Rainey: The Mother of the Blues." TheJaxsonMag.com, July 27, 2018. thejaxsonmag.com/article/ma-rainey-the-mother-of-the-blues

Ritz Theatre and Museum: Davis, Ennis, and Bill Delaney. "Inside the Ritz Theater and Museum." TheJaxsonMag.com, August 6, 2020. thejaxsonmag.com/article/inside-the-ritz-theatre-and-museum

Lift Ev'ry Voice and Sing Park: Birthplace of an Anthem: Davis, Ennis. "Lift Ev'ry Voice and Sing Park Renderings." TheJaxsonMag.com, October 1, 2020. thejaxsonmag.com/article/lift-evry-voice-and-sing-park-renderings; Delaney, Bill. "The History of Lift Ev'ry Voice and Sing." TheJaxsonMag.com, February 12, 2020. thejaxsonmag.com/article/the-history-of-lift-evry-voice-and-sing; Delaney, Bill. "The Harp: Augusta Savage's Lost Masterpiece." TheJaxsonMag.com, February 12, 2021. thejaxsonmag.com/article/the-harp-augusta-savages-lost-masterpiece

Clara White Mission: Davis, Ennis. "The Remains of Jax's Ragtime, Blues and Jazz Age." ModernCities.com, December 4, 2017. moderncities.com/article/2017-dec-the-remains-of-jaxs-ragtime-blues-and-jazz-age; Davis, Ennis, and Kristen Pickrell. "Ma Rainey, the Mother of the Blues." TheJaxsonMag.com, July 27, 2018. thejaxsonmag.com/article/ma-rainey-the-mother-of-the-blues; Davis, Ennis. "Dr. Martin Luther King, Jr. Sites in Jacksonville." TheJaxsonMag.com, January 18, 2021. thejaxsonmag.com/article/dr-martin-luther-king-jr-sites-in-jacksonville

The Whetstonian: Gilmore, Tim. "LaVilla: The Whetstonian's Last Days?" TheJaxsonMag.com, February 2, 2017. thejaxsonmag.com/article/lavilla-the-whetstonians-last-days; Strickland, Sandy. "Curious Jax: The Whetstonian Was His Smithsonian." *The Florida Times-Union*, February 17, 2020. jacksonville.com/story/news/local/2020/02/17/curious-jax-whetstonian-was-his-smithsonian/112248714

Sally Dark Rides: King, Kerry. "The Ride of His Life: John Wood ('74) brings the Magic of Dark Rides to Amusement Parks around the World" *Wake Forest Magazine*, May 11, 2017. magazine.wfu.edu/2017/05/11/the-ride-of-his-life; Szakonyi, Mark. "Sally Corp. Scares Up Profits on Dark Rides." *Jacksonville Business Journal*. October 24, 2007. bizjournals.com/jacksonville/stories/2007/10/29/story4.html; White, Tyler. "Making Memories in the Dark: Inside Sally Corp's Banner Year." *Jacksonville Business Journal*, August 9, 2019. bizjournals.com/jacksonville/news/2019/08/09/making-memories-in-the-dark-inside-sally-corps.html

Laura Adorkor Kofi Mausoleum: Newman, Richard. "'Warrior Mother of Africa's Warriors of the Most High God': Laura Adorkor Kofi and the African Universal Church." *This Far by Faith: Readings in African-American Women's Religious Biography*, edited by Judith Weisenfeld and Richard Newman, Routledge, 2014.

Cat House: **The Jaguar Mural:** Banas, Anne. "Anne Banas' 'Cat House.'" AnneBanas.com, 2014. annebanas.com/cathouse.htm; Patton, Charlie. "Iconic Jaguar Mural Moving to Weaver Center for Community Outreach." *The Florida Times-Union*, September 23, 2015. jacksonville.com/article/20150903/NEWS/801252481

Zora Neale Hurston in the First Coast: Boyd, Valerie. *Wrapped in Rainbows: The Life of Zora Neale Hurston*. Scribner, 2004; Davis, Ennis. "Six Zora Neale Hurston Sites in Jacksonville." TheJaxsonMag.com, March 18, 2021. thejaxsonmag.com/article/six-zora-neale-hurston-sites-in-jacksonville

Big Jim: Bloch, Emily. "Big Jim's Back, Steam Whistle Repaired." *The Florida Times-Union*, September 12, 2019, jacksonville.com/news/20190912/big-jims-back-steam-whistle-repaired; Strickland, Sandy. "Call Box: Jacksonville's 'Oldest City Employee' Still Bellowing Four Times a Day." *The Florida Times-Union*, April 11, 2016, jacksonville.com/article/20160411/NEWS/801246333;Tsai, Monica. "A Change in Plans: JEA Adjusting Plans for Springfield Museum." *The Jacksonville Daily Record*, December 19, 2003, jaxdailyrecord.com/article/change-plans; Wood, Wayne W., Stephen Joseph Tool Jr., and Joel Wright McEachin. *Jacksonville's Architectural Heritage*. University Press of Florida, 1996.

Karpeles Manuscript Library Museum: Patton, Charlie "Get It Documented." *The Florida Times-Union*, January 21, 2001; Patton, Charlie. "Jacksonville's Karpeles Manuscript Library Museum Has the Write Stuff." *The Florida Times-Union*, March 1, 2011; Wood, Wayne W., Stephen Joseph Tool Jr., and Joel Wright McEachin. *Jacksonville's Architectural Heritage*. University Press of Florida, 1996.

Garlic Crabs: Bill, and Katie Delaney. "Garlic Crabs: A Rich (and Buttery) Local Tradition." *Edible Northeast Florida Magazine*. May/June 2021.

Evergreen Cemetery: History Written on the Tombstones: Delaney, Bill. "A Tour of Historic Evergreen Cemetery." TheJaxsonMag.com, October 27, 2020. thejaxsonmag.com/article/a-tour-of-historic-evergreen-cemetery

Thompson Williams's Grave—A Painful Secret: Davis, Ennis. "Erased: Jacksonville's Mount Herman Cemetery." TheJaxsonMag.com, February 19, 2020. thejaxsonmag.com/article/erased-jacksonvilles-mount-herman-cemetery; Soergel, Matt. "A Hero's Grave." *The Florida Times-Union*, 2021. static.jacksonville.com/files/1908/hero-s-grave-thompson-williams-story.html

Edward Waters University, Florida's Oldest HBCU: Davis, Ennis. "Exploring the Campus of Edward Waters College." TheJaxsonMag.com, January 6, 2021. thejaxsonmag.com/article/exploring-the-campus-of-edward-waters-college; Gilmore, Tim. "Edward Waters College, 2: Centennial Hall (and Salter)—Peering into the Vanished." JaxPsychoGeo.com, March 19, 2021. jaxpsychogeo.com/west/edward-waters-college-2-centennial-hall-and-salter-peering-into-the-vanished; Rivers, Larry Eugene, and Canter Brown Jr. *Laborers in the Vineyard of the Lord: The Beginnings of the AME Church in Florida, 1865–1895*. University Press of Florida, 2001.

J. P. Small Park—Home of Florida's First Major Leaguers: Delaney, Bill. "Felix Mantilla Helped Break Jax's Baseball Color Line." TheJaxsonMag.com, October 6, 2020. thejaxsonmag.com/article/felix-mantilla-helped-break-jaxs-baseball-color-line; Delaney, Bill. "The Jax Red Caps: Florida's First Major Leaguers." TheJaxsonMag.com, December 18, 2020. thejaxsonmag.com/article/the-jax-red-caps-floridas-first-major-leaguers

Holley's Bar B Q: Davis, Ennis. "Jacksonville's Oldest Local Barbecue Restaurants." TheJaxsonMag.com, May 11, 2020. thejaxsonmag.com/article/jacksonvilles-oldest-local-barbecue-restaurants

Moncrief Springs and White Harvest Farms: Meerschaert, Kevin. "White Harvest Farms Seeks to Bring Healthy Food to Moncrief." WJCT, February 28, 2014. news.wjct.org/post/white-harvest-farms-seeks-bring-healthy-food-moncrief; "White Harvest Farms." Clara White Mission, 2021, clarawhitemission.org/what-we-do/white-harvest-farms

Florida Native Bird Rookery at the Jacksonville Zoo: "Bird Watching at the Zoo." Jacksonville Zoo, 2021. jacksonvillezoo.org/bird-watching; Cravey, Beth. "Wood Storks to Be Removed from Endangered List after Rebound in Florida Nesting." *The Florida Times-Union*, December 26, 2012. jacksonville.com/article/20121226/NEWS/801241159

Devil's School: Haunted Annie Lytle Elementary: Davis, Ennis, and Robert Mann, *Reclaiming Jacksonville: Stories Behind the River City's Historic Landmarks*, Arcadia Publishing, 2012; Delaney, Bill. "Jaxlore: Folklore, Urban Legends, and Regionalisms." Metro Jacksonville, February 12, 2015. metrojacksonville.com/article/2015-feb-jaxlore-folklore-urban-legends-and-regionalisms

Sun-Ray Cinema: Soergel, Matt. "Renovation of Jacksonville's 5 Points Theatre Could Be Ready by Dec. 1." *The Florida Times-Union*, October 18, 2011.

Jiffy Feet Don't Fail Me Now: Delaney, Bill. "Jaxlore: Jiffy Feet—A Comprehensive History." TheJaxsonMag.com, April 28, 2020. thejaxsonmag.com/article/jaxlore-jiffy-feet-a-comprehensive-history

Willowbranch Park: Jacksonville's LGBTQ Holy Ground: Cravey, Beth Reese. "Jacksonville's Willowbranch Park Is 'Holy Ground' for AIDS Memorial." *The Florida Times-Union*, February 14, 2019. jacksonville.com/news/20190214/jacksonvilles-willowbranch-park-is-holy-ground-for-aids-memorial

Camel Riders: Deliciousness in a Pita: Davis, Ennis. "10 Long Time Arab American Businesses in Jacksonville." TheJaxsonMag.com, April 30, 2020. thejaxsonmag.com/article/10-long-time-arab-american-businesses-in-jacksonville; Delaney, Bill. "A Look at Jacksonville's Arab American Community." TheJaxsonMag.com, April 2, 2020. thejaxsonmag.com/article/a-look-at-jacksonvilles-arab-american-community; Edge, John T. "A Taste of Jacksonville, Tucked into a Pita." *The New York Times*, July 31, 2012. nytimes.com/2012/08/01/dining/in-jacksonville-camel-rider-sandwiches-are-ubiquitous.html

Gray House: Birthplace of the Allman Brothers Band, Southern Rock Pioneers: FitzGerald, Michael Ray. *Jacksonville and the Roots of Southern Rock*. University Press of Florida, 2021; Soergel, Matt. "Allman Brothers Band Began in Old House on Riverside Avenue." *The Florida Times-Union*, February 21, 2019. jacksonville.com/news/20190221/allman-brothers-band-began-in-old-house-on-riverside-avenue

St. Johns River Monster: Gilmore, Tim. "In Search of the St. Johns River Monster." TheJaxsonMag.com, September 9, 2020. thejaxsonmag.com/article/in-search-of-the-st-johns-river-monster

Treaty Oak—Jacksonville's Oldest Resident: Davis, Ennis. "The Story of Dixieland Park." TheJaxsonMag.com, July 5, 2016. thejaxsonmag.com/article/the-story-of-dixieland-park; Figart, Larry. "Jacksonville's Treaty Oak." A New Leaf, UF/IFAS Extension Duval County, May/June 2019. sfyl.ifas.ufl.edu/media/sfylifasufledu/duval/agriculture/newsletterssocialmedia/nleafMayJunel.19mail.pdf

St. Johns River Taxi and River Dolphins: Bauerlein, David. "Water Taxis Faring Better." *The Florida Times-Union*. October 29, 1999; "UNF Dolphin Research Program: Jacksonville's Urban Dolphins." University of North Florida, 2018. unfdolphins.domains.unf.edu

Marco Lake: Delaney, Bill. "Secret Jacksonville: Marco Lake." TheJaxsonMag.com, May 20, 2020. thejaxsonmag.com/article/hidden-jacksonville-marco-lake

***El Faro* Memorial:** Hong, Christopher. "Statue at Dames Point Park Will Honor Those Lost aboard the El Faro." *The Florida Times-Union*, September 23, 2016. jacksonville.com/news/metro/2016-09-23/story/statue-dames-point-park-will-honor-those-lost-aboard-el-faro; Schafer, Daniel. "Dames Point / Crosses Point." University of North Florida's Florida History Online, 2021. unf.edu/floridahistoryonline/Plantations/plantations/Dames_Point-Crosses_Point.htm

Kingsley Plantation: Delaney, Bill. "Old Red Eyes and the Ghosts of Kingsley Plantation." TheJaxsonMag.com, October 31, 2019. thejaxsonmag.com/article/old-red-eyes-and-the-ghosts-of-kingsley-plantation; Schafer, Daniel. *Anna Madgigine Jai Kingsley: African Princess, Florida Slave, Plantation Slaveowner*. University Press of Florida, 2010.

The Neff House and the Mysterious Betz Sphere: Delaney, Bill. "The Mysterious Betz Sphere of Fort George Island." TheJaxsonMag.com, October 20, 2019. thejaxsonmag.com/article/the-mysterious-betz-sphere-of-fort-george-island

Mission San Juan del Puerto: Hann, John H. *A History of the Timucua Indians and Missions*. University Press of Florida, 1996.

Blackrock Beach (Boneyard Beach): Florida Department of Environmental Protection. "Big Talbot Island State Parks Approved Multi-Unit Management Plan." June 13, 2008, floridadep.gov/sites/default/files/Amelia%20Island%20State%20Park%202008%20Approved%20Plan.pdf

American Beach: Florida's First Black-Owned Beach Resort: Phelts, Marsha Dean. *An American Beach for African Americans*. University Press of Florida, 1997; Rymer, Russ. "Beach Lady." *Smithsonian Magazine*, June 2003, smithsonianmag.com/history/beach-lady-84237022; National Parks Service. "American Beach Nana Sand Dune." February 2, 2021, nps.gov/places/american-beach-nana-sand-dune.htm; Jackson, Cindy. "Little Nana Dune System Saved for Now." *Fernandina Observer*, June 9, 2020, fernandinaobserver.com/county-news/little-nana-dune-system-saved-for-now

Old Town: The Original Location of Fernandina: "Fernandina Plaza Historic State Park." Florida State Parks, 2021. floridastateparks.org/parks-and-trails/fernandina-plaza-historic-state-park

Birthplace of Modern Shrimping: Edenfield, Gray. "Amelia Island: Birthplace of the Modern Shrimping Industry." America Through Time, November 19, 2014.

The Palace Saloon: Florida's Oldest Bar: Litrico, Helen Gordon. *The Palace: Where Ship Captains Gathered in the Days of the Tall Ships*. Land & Williams, 1994. ameliaisland.pastperfectonline.com/archive/694B7D3F-C25E-4718-B179-805870487768

Wiccademous, the Witch of Fernandina: Delaney, William. "Jaxlore: The Grave of Wiccademous." TheJaxsonMag.com, forthcoming.

Egans Creek Greenway: A Natural Refuge in the Heart of Fernandina Beach: Delaney, Bill. "A Walk Down Fernandina Beach's Egans Creek Greenway." TheJaxsonMag.com, February 4, 2021, thejaxsonmag.com/article/a-walk-down-fernandina-beachs-egans-creek-greenway

White Oak Conservation: "The Fall of The House of Gilman". *Forbes*, August 11, 2003. forbes.com/forbes/2003/0811/068.html?sh=625762552086; Davis, Ennis. "Exploring White Oak Conservation." Modern Cities, April 30, 2018. moderncities.com/article/2018-apr-exploring-white-oak-conservation; Stepzinski, Teresa. "First Group of Retired Circus Elephants Settle In at White Oak Conservation Near Jacksonville." *The Florida Times-Union*, April 30, 2021. jacksonville.com/story/lifestyle/nature-wildlife/2021/04/30/white-oak-conservation-near-jacksonville-retired-ringling-bros-barnum-and-bailey-circus-elephants/4879213001

Cumberland Island: "Center for State of the Parks: Cumberland Island National Seashore." National Parks Conservation Association. 2009; Hendrix, Steve. "On Cumberland Island, You Don't Have to Choose between Roughing It and Pampering Yourself." *The Washington Post*, November 19, 2015. washingtonpost.com/lifestyle/travel/on-cumberland-island-you-dont-have-to-choose-between-roughing-it-and-pampering-yourself/2015/11/19/c51d1952-8d56-11e5-934c-a369c80822c2_story.html

Okefenokee Swamp: Land of the Trembling Earth: Nelson, Megan Kate. *Trembling Earth: A Cultural History of the Okefenokee Swamp*. University of Georgia Press, 2009.

Bulls Bay Preserve and Waterfall: Delaney, Bill. "Secret Jacksonville: Bulls Bay Preserve and Waterfall." TheJaxsonMag.com, August 12, 2020. thejaxsonmag.com/article/secret-jacksonville-bulls-bay-preserve-and-waterfall

Camp Milton: "Camp Milton Historic Preserve." History Southeast, 2019. historysoutheast.com/campmilton; Schafer, Daniel L. *Thunder on the River: The Civil War in Northeast Florida*. University Press of Florida, 2010; Word, Ron. "Jacksonville's Camp Milton: A Little-Known Civil War Jewel." *Orlando Sentinel*, August 17, 2009. orlandosentinel.com/orl-travel-camp-milton-florida-story-story.html

Jacksonville's Southern Rock Graves: Delaney, Bill, and Chris Soldt. "Jacksonville's Southern Rock Graves." TheJaxsonMag.com, February 14, 2020. thejaxsonmag.com/article/jacksonvilles-southern-rock-graves

The Birthplace of the Blue Angels: "NAS Jax Air Show, the Birth of the Blue Angels in Jacksonville, FL." Fly Jacksonville, October 16, 2018. flyjacksonville.com/jetstream/nas-jax-air-show-the-birth-of-the-blue-angels-in-jacksonville-fl; "History of the Blue Angels." Blue Angels, 2021. blueangels.navy.mil/history; Smolinski, Johns. "NAS Jax CO Offers Tour of Heritage Park." *The Florida Times-Union*, May 6, 2015. jacksonville.com/article/20150506/NEWS/801244740

Yukon: Jacksonville's Ghost Town: Davis, Ennis. "Jacksonville's Ghost Town: Yukon." TheJaxsonMag.com, July 26, 2019. thejaxsonmag.com/article/jacksonvilles-ghost-town-yukon

Wreck of the *Maple Leaf*: Schafer, Daniel L. *Thunder on the River: The Civil War in Northeast Florida*. University Press of Florida, 2010.

Yerkes Laboratories of Primate Biology—Behold the Humanzee: Delaney, Bill. "Jaxlore: Orange Park's 'Monkey Farm' and the Humanzee." TheJaxsonMag.com, forthcoming; Gallup, Gordon. Personal interview, 2019.

Green Cove Spring Park: National Register of Historic Places: Green Cove Springs Historic District. National Park Service, 1991. npgallery.nps.gov/GetAsset/4d81c490-eb0a-4008-998d-8653504955f4

Bardin Booger: Delaney, Bill. "Jaxlore: Folklore, Urban Legends, and Regionalisms." Metro Jacksonville, February 12, 2015, metrojacksonville.com/article/2015-feb-jaxlore-folklore-urban-legends-and-regionalisms

Exchange Club Island (Mud Island): Field, Mike. "Big Changes Coming to Island Under Mathews Bridge." TheJaxsonMag.com, March 12, 2017. thejaxsonmag.com/article/big-changes-coming-to-island-under-mathews-bridge; Soergel, Matt. "Island under Mathews Bridge Has Colorful Past, Plans for Future." *The Florida Times-Union*, May 23, 2016. jacksonville.com/article/20160523/NEWS/801248467; Soergel, Matt. "Capt. Augustus Swan's Castaway's Life on St. Johns River Island." *The Florida Times-Union*, September 12, 2016. jacksonville.com/news/metro/2016-09-12/story/capt-augustus-swans-castaways-life-st-johns-river-island

Norman Studios and Silent Film's Winter Capital: Miller, Blair. *Almost Hollywood: The Forgotten Story of Jacksonville, Florida*. Hamilton Books, 2013.

Kona Skatepark, Skateboarding Mecca: Robertson, Les. "King of Kona: Interview with Martin Ramos." SkateSlate, December 11, 2015. skateslate.com/blog/2015/12/11/king-of-kona-interview-with-martin-ramos; Soergel, Matt. "Kona." *The Florida Times-Union*, July 1, 2007. Soergel, Matt. "Skateboarders Tell of Jacksonville's Old Days on Boards." *The Florida Times-Union*, June 16, 2010. jacksonville.com/article/20100616/ENTERTAINMENT/801250330

Cosmo and the Gullah Geechee Heritage Corridor: Bauerlein, David. "Commemorating Cosmo: New Jacksonville Park Highlights Community Founded by Freed Slaves." *The Florida Times-Union*, January 23, 2021. jacksonville.com/story/news/local/2021/01/24/new-jacksonville-park-spotlights-how-freed-slaves-formed-cosmo/6668829002/; Jones, David. "Living History: Freedom Park Will Memorialize Local Gullah Geechee People, Veterans with PTSD in Jacksonville." First Coast News, March 14, 2020. firstcoastnews.com/article/news/local/living-history-freedom-park-will-memorialize-local-gullah-geechee-people-veterans-with-ptsd-in-jacksonville/77-9a2ad817-1c33-4967-9f77-e57d48d3b766; Wilson, Cristin. "Remembering Cosmo: For About 100 Years, Families of Former Slaves Made a Life on East Arlington Land." *The Florida Times-Union*, January 18, 2015, jacksonville.com/article/20150118/NEWS/801237613

Hontoon Owl—The World's Largest Pre-Columbian Woodcarving: Milanich, Jerald T. *Archaeology of Pre-Columbian Florida*. University Press of Florida, 1994; Williamson, Ronald. "Hontoon Changeling: The Ancient Owl Carving That Represents the Wrong Tribe." Florida History Network, April 2003. floridahistorynetwork.com/hontoon-changling-the-ancient-owl-carving-that-represents-the-wrong-tribe.html

The Timucuan Preserve's Theodore Roosevelt Area—The Greatest Gift in Jacksonville History: Delaney, Bill. "Timucuan Preserve: A Walk through Willie Browne's Woods." TheJaxsonMag.com, January 22, 2021. thejaxsonmag.com/article/timucuan-preserve-a-walk-through-willie-brownes-woods

The Ribault Column: Gilmore, Tim. "Fort Caroline: Ribault Monument." Jax Psycho Geo, December 6, 2020. jaxpsychogeo.com/east/fort-caroline-ribault-monument

Spanish-American War Battery: Helmick, Gregory. "North Florida in the Cuban Literary Canon." *Southern Literary Journal*, Volume 46, Number 2, Spring 2014, pp. 45-66; Buker, George E. "Spanish American War Fortifications: St. Johns Bluff, Florida." Fort Caroline National Memorial, 1989. digitalcommons.unf.edu/cgi/viewcontent.cgi?article=1009&context=northeast_fla; Adan, Abukar. "National Park Service Receives Jacksonville Spanish American War Fort." WJCT, December 14, 2018. news.wjct.org/post/national-park-service-receives-jacksonville-spanish-american-war-fort-0

The Salaam Club and the Ramallah Club of Jacksonville: Delaney, Bill. "A Look at Jacksonville's Arab American Community." TheJaxsonMag.com, April 2, 2020. thejaxsonmag.com/article/a-look-at-jacksonvilles-arab-american-community

Sexy Rexy, King of Beach Boulevard: "Call Box: T. rex Lives Near Beach and Peach." *The Florida Times-Union*, December 29, 2012. jacksonville.com/article/20121229/NEWS/801241011; Mathis, Karen Brune. "This T-Rex Will Never Go Extinct." *The Florida Times-Union*, January 9, 2007. Mathis, Karen Brune. "Suggested Names Roar in for T-Rex." *The Florida Times-Union*, January 23, 2007.

Mussallem Galleries: Rugs, Fine Art and Antiquities: Kerr, Jessie-Lynne. "Charles Mussallem Jr.: 1925–2007." *The Florida Times-Union*, December 18, 2007; Mathis, Karen Brune. "Mussallem Lists Philips Highway Gallery for $11.2M." *Jacksonville Daily Record*, May 15, 2014; jaxdailyrecord.com/article/mussallem-lists-philips-highway-gallery-112m; Young, Marilyn. "UNF's Permanent Art Collection." *UNF Journal*, Winter 2019. issuu.com/jessicawingatedesigns/docs/winter_journal_2019

Harriet Beecher Stowe's Mandarin School: Delaney, Bill. "Writers of the First Coast: Harriet Beecher Stowe." TheJaxsonMag.com, April 21, 2020. thejaxsonmag.com/article/writers-of-the-first-coast-harriet-beecher-stowe; Nolan, Brett. "Back in Time with Brett | Mandarin Community Club." *Florida NewsLine*, November 26, 2019. floridanewsline.com/mandarin/back-in-time-with-brett-mandarin-community-club/#:~:text=By%201871%2C%20after%20mismanagement%20of,till%20it%20was%20no%20more

The Brumos Collection: Irwin, Austin. "Tour the Brumos Collection in Jacksonville, Florida." *Car and Driver*, March 12, 2020. caranddriver.com/features/g30783854/best-of-brumos-collection-jacksonville-florida; Macdonald, Dan. "The Brumos Collection: Opportunity Meets Racing History." *Jacksonville Daily Record*, February 14, 2020, jaxdailyrecord.com/article/the-brumos-collection-opportunity-meets-racing-history; sportscar365.com/imsa/brumos-closes-its-doors-haywood-reflects-on-legacy; Robinson, Aaron. "Brumos Collection Houses the History of Florida's Hometown Race Team." Hagerty, March 12, 2020. hagerty.com/media/automotive-history/brumos-museum-houses-the-history-of-floridas-hometown-race-team; Scanlan, Dan. "Filled with Iconic Racing Cars and Nostalgia, Brumos Opens Jacksonville Car Museum." *The Florida Times-Union*, January 21, 2020, jacksonville.com/story/news/local/2020/01/21/filled-with-iconic-racing-cars-and-nostalgia-brumos-opens-jacksonville-car-museum/112223710.

Beaches Museum: Reynolds, Tiffanie. "Piece of Old Palm Valley Finds Home with Beaches Museum." *The Florida Times-Union*, November 11, 2016. jacksonville.com/shorelines/2016-11-11/piece-old-palm-valley-finds-home-beaches-museum

The Jacksonville Beach Pier and the Birth of First Coast Surfing: "Jacksonville Beach Travel & Surf Guide." Surfline, 2021. surfline.com/travel/united-states/florida/duval-county/jacksonville-beach-surfing-and-beaches/4160023; Soergel, Matt. "By 1964, Beaches Became an Endless Summer as Everybody Went Surfing." *The Florida Times-Union*, March 25, 2019. jacksonville.com/news/20190325/by-1964-beaches-became-endless-summer-as-everybody-went-surfing; Hong, Christopher. "Jacksonville Beach Pier to Close for 2 Years to Repair Matthew Damage." *The Florida Times-Union*, August 2, 2019. jacksonville.com/news/20190802/jacksonville-beach-pier-to-close-for-2-years-to-repair-matthew-damage; Longnecker, Bill. "Wavelengths: Local Beaches Have Special Place in Surfing Lore." Shorelines, March 22, 2020. jacksonville.com/story/lifestyle/shorelines/2020/03/26/wavelengths-local-beaches-have-special-place-in-surfing-lore/41822247

Alpha Paynter, Ghost of TacoLu: Delaney, Bill. "Jaxlore: Folklore, Urban Legends, and Regionalisms." Metro Jacksonville, February 12, 2015, metrojacksonville.com/article/2015-feb-jaxlore-folklore-urban-legends-and-regionalisms; Mabry, Daniel. "The Alpha O. Paynter Mystery." 2014, Academia, academia.edu/11574555/The_Alpha_O_Paynter_Mystery

Mayport Village: Johnson, Jeff. *Shrimp Highway: Savoring US 17 and Its Iconic Dish*. McFarland, 2017; Wood, Wayne W., Stephen Joseph Tool Jr., and Joel Wright McEachin. *Jacksonville's Architectural Heritage*. University Press of Florida, 1996.

Beluthahatchee: Stetson Kennedy's Home: FitzRoy, Maggie. "St. Johns County Preserving Historic Literary Landmark" *The Florida Times-Union*, February 9, 2013.

St. Johns County's Ghost Light Road: Delaney, Bill. "Jaxlore: The Erstwhile Ghost Light of Greenbriar Road." TheJaxsonMag.com, October 28, 2020. thejaxsonmag.com/article/jaxlore-the-erstwhile-ghost-light-of-greenbriar-road

Datil Peppers: Friese, Kurt Michael, Kraig Kraft, and Gary Paul Nabhan. *Chasing Chiles: Hot Spots Along the Pepper Trail*. Chelsea Green Publishing, 2011.

Castle Otttis: Smith, Wes. "One Man's Castle." *Orlando Sentinel*, July 12, 2005. orlandosentinel.com/news/os-xpm-2005-07-12-castle12-story.html

Secrets of the Fountain of Youth: *Landing of Ponce de Leon*. National Park Service, May 1929. npshistory.com/publications/proposed-parks/fl-fountain-of-youth-nm.pdf; thesecret.pbworks.com/w/page/120834408/Image%206%20Verse%209%20Solution

The Hurricane Lady: Donges, Patrick, and Bill Carter. "Meet the Centuries-Old Statue Some Say Protects St. Augustine from Hurricanes." WJCT, July 1, 2014. news.wjct.org/post/meet-centuries-old-statue-some-say-protects-st-augustine-hurricanes; Lane, Marcia. "Benet Family Thread Tightly Woven in Tapestry of Time." *The St. Augustine Record*, August 12, 2013. staugustine.com/article/20130812/NEWS/308129987

Fort Mose: Blumetti, Jordan. "The First Floridians." Bitter Southerner, 2021. bittersoutherner.com/the-first-floridians-fort-mose-st-augustine; Davis, Ennis. "Six Free Black Towns in Florida." TheJaxsonMag.com, April 14, 2020. thejaxsonmag.com/article/six-free-black-towns-in-florida

Marineland: Brotemarkle, Ben. "Florida Frontiers: Marineland of Florida." *Florida Frontiers*, May 3, 2017. myfloridahistory.org/frontiers/article/162

INDEX